ASSES AND GINGER ROOTS

Musings of an Artist from the Middle East, Europe, and America

by
Ano Ertas

ACKNOWLEDGEMENTS

All quotations are from cultural and historical observations, embedded memoirs, residues and collections of memories as of a blessed and lucky student of the first American schools opened in the Ottoman Empire by a very smart American President, Thomas Jefferson. Talas American School, in Kayseri, Turkey and Tarsus American College in Saint Paul's hometown, Tarsus. Later observations and notations were imbedded through lectures of very educated and multilingual environment of the Department of Philology, Istanbul University, Istanbul, Turkey.

I do thank my educators and mentors who sculpted my future through universal importance of the arts on developing proper human values for productive healthy joyous human interaction.

In the course of my travels and lectures, I have been asked by many, how I could leave behind all that was given to me to be enjoyed and shared by others for a better enlightenment, productive, loving and peaceful human interaction.

From the bottom of my heart I would like to extend my sincerest thanks to all artists and literary minds that helped me enjoy and share their wisdom and gifts. The responsibility for any imperfect recollections is mine alone.

CONTENTS

UNDUE ACCESSIBILITY TO THE UNCULTURED WASTE MANAGEMENT?

Quaereris quo jaceas post abitum loco?
Quo non nata jasent.

Seneca

What is your destination when you die?
Will join those who have not yet been born.

An alert traveler to this day can hear and appreciate the wisdom of the passed Mesopotamian cultures that resonated their universal observation through philosophy and the algebraic modes for better appreciation of any form of communal social and economic accessibility.

They passed on their observations and wisdom not through heavy and hard to process lexicon and mode of delivery exercised by contemporary schools of philosophy but through simple anecdotal and humorous mannerism which was referred to as "Wisdom through the back door."

"My child do not ever forget that,

> *He who knows not and knows not that he knows not,*
> *He is a fool, shun him;*
> *He who knows not and knows he knows not,*
> *He is simple, teach him;*
> *He who knows and knows not he knows,*
> *He is asleep, wake him;*
> *He who know and knows he knows,*
> *He is wise; follow him."*

Arabian proverb

In the course of our communal engagements we often heard that in the mathematical arena any number, no matter how great, if multiplied by zero would always stay zero. Thusly it was explained to us that, if one never leaves his ground zero of life, appreciation of anything served to him will have zero impact on his presence.

As time hauls away the used and the unused it never fails to constantly bring new elements to one's door that might be put to use to enhance the formation and in the preparedness for healthy and tasteful life engagements. However the developing young mind should be taught early in this formation that its responsibility to open the door and bring all he or she can of that which was brought to their doors and be put to cultavative use that is delivered in a timely fashion.

"They shall be drunk with the plenty of thy house"

St Thomas Aquinas

How did Saint Thomas Aquinas prophesy the decadence of times to come so far in advance? Was it because he was a holy spiritualist? Was he a reader of tea leaves? I do not think so! He simply looked at the past history and observed the traveled paths of decadent self-centered inquisitors and their destined doom

Do we trace any similarities between the cultures of the past that led the way onto the path of extinction from the world map and ours as the leading culture around the globe today? I am deeply troubled to say, "Very much so!"

If you do not believe this observation, the next time you leave your home, pretend to be an artist in any field, visual, literary or audio and try to seek a subject matter around you that could be of universal concern. Don't forget, you are the observer, processor, and reporter without being an editor. See if you notice any subject matter that may be reviewed as a norm with some hidden virus within your communal culture at large that Saint Thomas Aquinas might classify as socially corrosive.

As a visual artist I will start by touching on an issue that has affected humanity from creation. To learn to appreciate the essentials through the process of proper entry into the social composition one could eliminate waste in any form. Waste is the end product of neglect and untimely access to all givens. Almost all faiths have given examples of abuses of God's gifts by many in history. So how does one really put to use the necessary elements to appreciate what was presented or served to one?

One can never appreciate and spiritually respond to a highly delicate elating human delivery if one has not developed the senses to aesthetically cogitate with it. Undue accessibility to the undeveloped mind and unrefined taste is nothing more than waste. This is why the title "Asses and Ginger Roots." This is a rough translation from an old Aramaic Idiom, "Ihmieer u'irk zencefil." Basically it means that the taste of a jackass can never surpass the taste of hay. That is to say, "it is a waste to serve a jackass ginger roots," a most sought after spice of past ages of limited resources, which is highly nutritious, healing, and tasty, for only those who have worked hard to develop a taste to appreciate it.

A lot of eastern cultures have very similar proverbs that they make sure a child hears and understands early in life. In western Asia of Turkish cultures almost all know the saying, "Putting a golden saddle on a Jackass will never make him a horse."

So what are the necessary and essential elements to live a fulfilled life? What are the avenues to maximize the appreciation of the undetermined time and space allocated to each in this earthly visit?

A young philosopher, humanist, Picco della Mirandola, in 1486 summed up his observations in his oration,

"On the Dignity of Man.

On sublime generosity of God the Father! Oh highest and most important felicity of Man! To him it was granted to be what he wills. The father endowed him with the seeds of every way of life. Whatever seed each man cultivates will germinate, grow and bear fruit within him. Who then will not wonder at this chameleon, man, who was said by Aeschylus of Athens able to transform his own nature owing to his mutability, and who is symbolized in the mysteries as Prometheus?"

My Life Overture

I sit here
Alone and
Await
With all I have
At the main gate
For that right one
To arrive
Hopefully not
Too late
And not just to pass by

With no artificial tie
but

Stop
Sit and share
From a heart
That is fair
The beauties
That surrounds us
With tender
Loving care
Take the needed time
To taste and learn to enjoy
So to reflect with no lie
With vested assurance to
Testify
That we really were here
Before we bade for eternal
Good-bye.

Ano

"Minutatim vires at robur adultum
Frangit et in pertem pejoreum liquitur oates"

Lucretius

"Time morbidly wears out
all who have reached age of maturity"

Differing mildly from the Roman philosopher, Lucretius and his admirer, sixteen-century freethinker, Montaigne's point of view of life in which he believed that, as we grow older and as days pass we drift away from our real self. Our identity begins to diminish gradually. Well, in the course of my lifetime, I have come to believe that time gradually drags us to our true self. Those who have consciously and truthfully participated in their self-growth might be blessed to arrive at the address of who they were destined to be. Early in life we have to be taught not to imitate but emulate those who we think have achieved social credibility. We should respect and learn from those who have located their truthful selfness by going through life and learning to distinguish through experience, the good, the bad and the ugly.

As I travel throughout the world, I believe, due to being an artist with an undistinguishable diction and unclassified visual delivery, somehow those I encounter feel more comfortable in bringing up issues for discussion that are of universal concern. Because of this, I myself often feel at ease and attuned in receiving and reflecting a more multidimensional world view, not just with others like myself but also of those who do not have the privilege of exercising physical presence. I have come to realize the importance of the arts as a major catalyst in productive and engaging human interaction. It is the belief of many retired thinkers and students of true aesthetics that a good piece of artwork, whether visual, literary, or auditory, should relay the true identity of complex human experience in a gently engaging manner for the main purpose of human betterment. Thusly I would like to share some of the wisdom through the tragic and comic experiences of the past time-travelers from whom I have vastly benefited.

If I had the privilege of enjoying a cup of wine in a café with Socrates, Mevlana, Lucretius or Montaigne, I am sure no matter what the subject matter of discussion was, we would arrive to the same courtyard of true human values from different gates. So my friends if you really want to enjoy and validate this brief visit to this planet, have your shoes ready to go on a search of your hidden true possibilities and vested endowments.

LOVE OF INQUIRY

"I prefer the folly of enthusiasm to the indifference of wisdom."

Anatole France

"Fortune favors the prepared mind."

A Jewish Proverb

GIFTS

Give a man a horse he can ride,
Give a man a boat he can sail;
And his rank and wealth,
His strength and health,
On sea nor shore shall fail.

Give a man a pipe he can smoke,
Give a man a book he can read;
And his home is bright with calm delight
Though the room be poor indeed.

> *Give a man a girl he can love*
> *As I, o my love, love thee;*
> *And his heart is great with pulse of faith*
> *At home, on land, on sea.*

James Thomson

It is very ironic that I, who in the course of all my adult life have advocated the love of inquiry into the unknown and through the path laid by past thinkers who dedicated their lives to study and share their wisdom in the course of their worldly wonderings, spent three years of my teenage years a block away from the house of the Apostle Paul, in Tarsus, Turkey. I could not have thought that this advocator of human engagement had declared war on the wisdom of the wise. Love for wisdom, "Philo Sophus," was considered by him a heretical act. Even the advocates of spiritual guides such as St. Thomas Aquinas in his book "Summa Contra Gentiles." As summary of the case against the heretics, any earthly thought processed by any thinker was declared a sin. However I have come to believe that it is very important to thank the traveler, Apostle Paul of Tarsus, for his admirable efforts to take upon himself the harsh and demanding task by taking many unpredictable risks of the times to travel into unknown lands to share his spiritual quest and spreading the message advocated by a Jewish street preacher that lay the foundation for true humanism.

There is no doubt in my mind that in the course of Paul's voyage on these unknown paths he learned much more about the importance of social humanism then when he was just a Roman tax bureaucrat. However it is also essential that we make use of the God-given wisdom that advocates the importance of truth so we may be able to make our share of contribution while on this visit into humanity. How else can we bring home to share and appreciate all earthly resources and lay the fruitful paths for coming generations if we do not make the effort to advocate the love of inquiry into the mysteries of darkness?

Alexander, the son of Philip II, the ruler of Macedonia, somehow must have been influenced by his tutor no other then one of the students of Plato, the Greek Philosopher Aristotle, to put on his shoes and go into other lands to seek alternate possibilities. Maybe he decided to see for himself if his mentor's observation about truth was justifiable when he heard his mentor say, "The investigation of the truth is in one way difficult, in another easy. An indication of this is found in the fact that no one is able to attain the truth adequately, while, on the other hand, no one fails entirely, but everyone says something true about the nature of things, and while individually they contribute little or nothing to the truth, by the union of all, a considerable amount is amassed."

The only way we as humans could satisfy the inner desire to seek the true values of all that is availed by our Creator, it is essential that each take part in going out and bringing back at least one brick to lay to the truthful human foundation.

ALWAYS HAVE YOUR SHOES READY

"A Journey of thousand paces always begins with a single step."

Chinese Proverb

"Even if you a seeker not
With us
You can still follow
And search the lands of Lot
Even if you a singer and a dancer not
Come play with us
Singing and dancing
Will in your life
Make a happy communal start."

Sufi Mevlana Celaleddin Rumi

Early in life every child has to be taught to overcome the fear of the unknown. One could truly enjoy all life resources if one develops the sense of inquisitiveness. When I was a young boy I remember the father of a friend told a little story to his son who never wanted to do anything. He did not like school, listening to the teachers and he always had an excuse for not doing his homework. He never liked to go anywhere even with his dad or mom to events in different parts of town. He always said that he was not ready. He had absolutely no enthusiasm for anything and constantly complained about how stupid and boring life was. The story was about children like him who lacked enthusiasm to venture into many roads of life of many possibilities and this village Sufi (Wise Man) Nasraddin Hoca.

In a small village in central Anatolia, kids like him were complaining about the demands their parents were putting upon them to get out and learn to do things so they could be self-sufficient when they grew up. When they complained that there was not much to learn the parents always mentioned the town Sufi, Nasreddin. They told them that he, the famous Nasraddin, who many from all around the country came to consult for wisdom, was born here in this same village that they complained about. So one day the children got together and talked about confronting this Wise Man to find out how he got to be so wise and so knowledgeable about life; that even their parents had to solicit him for advice.

So they all went to the dirt road that led to his little house and waited for an opportune moment to encounter him and ask him how he got to be so wise. When they saw him coming they ran towards him and one of them, Metin, who had the courage to confront him politely asked, "Honorable Hoca Nasreddin, my friends here and I want to really know how being born in a boring village like ours that you came to be so wise? We would really like to know. We promise we won't tell any one if you just tell us. We will keep it a secret; we promise." The Wise Man looked at them and said, "No, no, it's all right; you can tell others. It really is not a secret. See, actually it is not me; it's my shoes. See these shoes I have on they just love to go places." The children looked at each other and thought he was crazy. They have shoes too, but theirs never talked to them and asked them to go anywhere, do anything. Are shoes really why they know nothing about life? So they began to talk about this strange pair of shoes the old man had.

One of them had an idea. He said, "Well, we will have to find a way to trick him and get his shoes of wisdom and we are set for life." The boys waited for an opportune moment and one day as he was coming down the path they called to him, "Master, we were discussing with admiration your worldly knowledge but not quite so sure of your physical abilities. We were betting about your strength versus your wisdom. With all that you have got, Ali, here bets that you can not climb this Cyprus tree. Gazne and I bet that you can." He walked towards them and looked up at this tree and looked at them and said, "Well, let me see which one of you is right." He studied the tree for a moment and began to take off his shoes. They were all excited looking at his shoes that they were targeting to steal. But to their surprise the old sage began to stuff the shoes into his pockets of the shalvart, the old baggy tribal pants. They could not believe what he was doing. Murat, the instigator of the plan asked him, "Sir, do you want us to hold the shoes for you so it will be easier to climb?" Sensing of what they were up to, the wise elder replied, "Thanks a lot kids for your kind offer; but I think I should take them with me in case they might want to walk a new road that might be up there that has not been traveled on."

They all looked at each other as if to say, "Is this the Wise Man everyone came to for advice and consul? There is definitely something wrong here!"

HOW LONG WILL IT TAKE ME TO GET THERE?

Does it really matter?

"Let me fly away says little birdie,
Mother let me fly away."

Alfred Lord Tennyson

Many cultures throughout time have tried to educate through humor or anecdotal channeling the inquisitive but hesitant minds of their communities. The message they passed on to their children was that it is not the length of time to arrive at one's wished destination that mattered the most but the experience of surprising encounters on the way that nourished and matured the mind for better appreciation of life.

A story is told to children in the Middle East about a young man who had absolutely no interest of leaving his village and going to places where he might get a better sense of life possibilities. He finally developed enough courage and decided to go to this particular town where he was told that he may learn plenty from the many colorful migrating caravans that come routinely from different villages of different cultural orientation and share stories picked up in the course of their nomadic travels. He filled his bag with some bread and water and set on his way. Having been used to the heat of the desert he walked as fast as he could taking advantage of any shady path to avoid the need for water. He was not on the road for very long when he saw an old man coming from a side path heading in the same direction. He looked at the man and asked, "Hey old man; how long will it take me to get to the village Siverek?" The old man displayed no response but kept on walking. The young man thinking the old man did not hear him inquired again. The old man kept on walking without saying anything. The young man thinking he may be deaf or possibly handicapped gave up and got back on his track towards the village. He had not been on the road for long when he heard the old man trailing him with a very crackley but soft aged voice, "You will be there before sunset." The young man could not believe that the man had heard him but wondered why he had not displayed the courtesy of recognition thusly, turned to him and asked, "Old man I asked you hours ago twice, how come you did not answer me?" The Old man responded, "I could not answer you for I had to see the pace and enthusiasm of your walk before I could give you the proper and accurate response. But young man you don't have to worry about when you will get there for you have already met your first encounter with one of whom who has been there."

"Fear not that life shall come to an end, but rather fear that it shall never have a beginning."

J. H. Newman

"EVERY WISH IS LIKE A PRAYER WITH GOD"

Elizabeth Barrett Browning

"When we do the best we can, we never know what miracle is wrought in our life or the life of another"

Helen Keller

Since prosperity is nothing but a state of mind it presents itself in many forms. One should not wait for the passing waves of circumstances to be propelled forward. I recall a friend's father telling my buddy, that those who are ready will take advantage of the road to wisdom and happiness when opportunity presents itself. The rest will always complain that fortune never knocked on their doors. God never answers their prayers or grants them their wishes. Growing in a culture whose faith was imbedded in a higher spiritual power maintained by relatively apolitical institutions and spiritualists we were told early in life that we have to participate in earning all that we wish for. Thusly, fortune always prefers the prepared mind.

Once I heard a church elder say that a chain is only as strong as its weakest link. We must recognize that each one of us is only a link in the long chain of a social structure. If that is so, then it is for the collective benefit that we make sure we strengthen all we are linked to through sharing all that we each have benefited from.

"Try to leave footprints in the path that you wish people to follow and benefit."

An Arabic proverb

Now I am at a phase of my life where I feel an inherent obligation to share some of the wisdom that has been passed on to me through the simple process of social and cultural inheritance through the roads traveled in my shoes. As I am approaching the main gate and prepare to gracefully exit and enter into the coming phase of my soul, I will try to empty the basket that contains all that I have acquired in the course of my visit here in this life arena. I hope anyone who goes through the dump of this spiritual, cultural and social residue will find some value in what they pick and hopefully share it with those who may be in search of the same before the generally practiced discard.

In the course of my visit here, I have come to believe that what we call life is merely a brief trip, just like one takes on a train or a bus to go visit relatives who live in some unknown land. On the way, those who are awake will enjoy the most of what they perceive all composed of material and spiritual elements. Fortunate are those who in the course of this trip learn to gracefully channel the experience of human love into a passage to devine union. Well, I will try to make my channeling as simple as possible so any child or adult will find something not only of interest but also of social use.

TIME "THE MASTER CARVER"

One day in my prep school I heard a teacher tell us that no one on earth can reform himself without pain and suffering. Because he is both the stone and the carver.

Singula de nobis anni proedandur euntes

Horatius

"Years tear away some from all as they flow away"

Many, even before the time of Horatius, believed that time steals and drags away a part of us but in reality history has proven to us that time like the law of gravity has been the most trustworthy of all forces of nature. Properly handled, time will take away all that has been discarded but also provide all that is necessary in the duration of our formation.

Time to me is like a chisel and hammer in the hands of sculptors that carve away and give us, from blocks of stones, shape and form, from the time of delivery to the ordained studio, to our final exit from this life. The by product thusly is nothing more than the total investment of the carvers' education, spirit and the cultural resources they have inherited from their ancestral sculptors. We end up to be the final art product of those who directly and indirectly helped to form us. Thusly we should not claim all the achievements. However mildly different from the block of stone which has no power to select its carvers a human being is privileged to do part of the work himself by selecting and working with the carvers. Our birth givers are our first studio associates. We come to this world with vast resources of elements hidden in this bundle of six or seven pounds of that special delivery called birth. The studio or workshop that we were delivered into may have the tools and elements accessible to those who ordered this bundle. They may have access to all the worldly resources but may lack the spirit. Others may have absolutely no worldly goods but highly refined senses and spirit acquired by their previous carvers and composers. The irony is that the most necessary elements for one's proper input and appreciation of life are within the delivered package and are free. The key phrase here is "proper appreciation." The package has arrived. There seems to be no visible damage. Now which hands are equipped to open the package; check the content; and begin to assemble the givens without enclosed instructions? Who will help make use of all in that package before they go as discard for time to haul away?

Our Life Space

In my life space
I look around
With gentle and earthly pace
Enjoy all found

Gracefully review
All in the round

As a humane carver
As we all are

As one to other
Not so afar

Enhancing the soul
Hopefully
With no heavy toll

Wishing to find
The heavenly seed

Planted within each
To gently feed

In the depths.
Yet within our reach
Of the inner spirit
For all to harvest
So we enhance
Nicely
As one
To other
Whether foe
Or brother

Ano

CLEAN THE MIRROR

Master deflecting the negative and reflecting the positive.

To be able to cultivate the colorful seeds that are waiting for germination within us, it is imperative to seek the inherent gifts to clearly reflect the true inner self. If one early in life were taught that for these seeds to properly germinate and grow to bear the fruits for everyone to enjoy, one would eliminate the fear of proper social entry to the stage of humanity.

We can begin with the most obvious, the excellently placed sensory receptors. Without their educated interaction, the intelligence-processing center, the brain, is of no use. However it is essential to start any human engagement with a very clean and purified heart. Since the creation of man, the heart has been the real center of true reflections. Thusly all spiritual leaders of all times have preached that all who truly want to enjoy and appreciate the image of all life compositions have the responsibility to polish the mirrors of their inner spirit. The true beauty and message of any art form is not determined by its size but the true reflection of its content.

Once upon a time an Ottoman sultan was interviewing artists from different lands and different cultures to rehab two adjacent chambers in his Topkapi Palace, in Constantinople. Of the two finalists, one was from China and the other from Greece. To secure the commission the Greek told the sultan that history has recorded that his culture has been the most truly expressive of human values and beauties through the hands and hearts of Greek artists. The Chinese responded that history has shown that they not only possess all the necessary skills but also they have, through the centuries, developed the best spiritual reflective sense. Well, the Sultan offered both the challenge and gave each a chamber that was only separated by a curtain.

The Greek came fully equipped with hundreds of colors, mosaic, metals and gems. The Chinese artist came only with some buffing cloth and polish. After months of work they announced that they were ready for the Sultan's review. The Sultan arrived and first entered the chamber painted by the Greek artist. He was fascinated by the most beautiful creative and engaging work he saw. Then he asked his aid to open the curtains of the adjacent chamber. He was stunned with what he encountered. The Chinese, no more than a master craftsman, had done nothing but had masterfully buffed and polished the walls of his commissioned chamber. The engagingly reflective images of all the fabulous Greek artist's work upon the most elegantly cleansed and polished walls by the Chinese artist impressed the Sultan so deeply that he assigned him as the chief palace artist. Thusly in the Middle Eastern cultures there is always a reminder to those who edit and market what others have experienced as their own. "Do not do the talking but learn to truthfully and elegantly reflect with no editing, the life beauties experienced by those who did the walking." To be able to do that the least you can do is to clean and polish the inner walls of your heavenly designated spiritual chambers.

The best way to enjoy life it is to develop an organic atelier where one can use the available elements to minimize waste of availed human resources. If one does not have the means to create he is inherent with the resources within and all he has to do is to learn to deflect the negative and reflect the positive.

TASTE: NOT FOR SALE;
EDUCATE YOUR SENSES

What is "Good?"
What is "Bad?"

Haec perinde sunt, ut illius animus qui eu possident
Qui uti scit, ei bona illi qui non uttitur recte mala

Terentius

"Value of all vary by recipient
If it harms – bad;
If it benefits – good"

How can one learn to distinguish between "Good" and "Bad" and not confuse it with often loosely used form of evaluation, "Like" and "Dislike?" Here is one rule to remember about all forms of life mode of evaluation. LIKE OR DISLIKE IS PERSONAL. GOOD OR BAD IS UNIVERSAL. What one likes or dislikes will never exceed the level of one's state of taste. Good is good is good. Bad is bad is bad. So it is natural for one with bad taste to display appreciation of something that is essentially bad. So then it is our responsibility to find the ways and means to educate our senses to distinguish between good and bad.

Since taste can never be inherited or acquired with tangible assets like money and power, man has to be very grateful that the school of REFINED TASTE is pro-bono, free and open to everyone who wishes to register. But it is highly essential that one go through all proper phases to educate the senses.

One day, shortly after a review of some artwork during my first visit to America, I heard someone utter a commonly used expression that "beauty is only in the eyes of the beholder." Well it needs not even be mentioned. Of course one cannot perceive and appreciate the perception more then one's receptive capacity. But here is the problem. Many of us do not take the time to cultivate our senses so we can absorb and properly respond to the given. Real appreciation can only manifest itself when all that was served was elegantly and timely recognized; and I would like to emphasize "timeliness." Why -- because timely appreciation credits the facilitator. We shall look into the importance of proper response to a giver when we later talk about principles of human engagement.

Our delivery agency, or Creator, gave us not only a processing center, the brain, but the necessary receptors, visual, audio, touch, smell, taste and many others not so obvious, in such strategic locations so we can perceive all in the round, not just from one direction alone. When one remarks of being well-rounded, I hope they mean that a person is well-cultured. The culture I was raised in did not equate the expression of "well-read" with "well-rounded." That meant that one could be equipped and accessed with all the worldly academic data but if he has not been introduced to proper processing all that academically acquired through experience and mastering the art of human engagements, he still is hard-edged and considered not yet well-rounded.

"Vivit, et est vitae nescius ipse suae."

Ovidius

He is alive but does not know he is living.

23

SOFTEN UP

Be ready for proper human engagement. "We live to discover beauty. All else is a form of waiting."

Khalil Gibran

Learning the ways and means of gentle entry into an enjoyable social format.

To learn to perceive, process, and properly respond to what is given or transmitted to us we have to be involved in and partake in our self-creativity. You sometimes hear that someone is a well-rounded person. What does that really mean?

"El kiteb tarbi el tadwir"

Jeh'az

"The book of enlightenment and wisdom of the square and the round"

One sometimes wonders in the course of human history if some conflicts among cultures are indeed ordained not to hurt but to help better humanity. It seems incomprehensible to imagine of twelfth-century Spain as the intellectual center of our planet if it were not for the Muslim Andealusian Amewies of North Africa who had crossed the Iberian Peninsula and brought with them to share their cultural treasures. Imagine this was an era when Europe was coming out of centuries-old economic and cultural chaos. Their highly literary leaders reintroduced them to the centuries-old Greek and Mesopotamian cultural wealth. Contrary to today's belief, the Muslim invaders had better understanding of interactive ethics.

It is ironic that those so called invaders sponsored all sects and denominations to collaborate in making tremendous contribution in the arts and sciences such as astronomy, physics, chemistry, mathematics, and logic. They also introduced to the European culture the rational legal bureaucracy, which was not very well received by the restrictive European Christian hierarchy with its highly restrictive learning which was confined to a few monasteries and religious schools.

Because of the invaders initiative acts through translation of manuscripts from ancient Mesopotamian cultures such as Aramaic, Hebrew, and Arabic to Aegean Greek the grounds needed for the seeds of humanism to bear the fruit of enlightenment were cultivated.

"El kiteb tarbi el tadwir," "The Scripts of Enlightenment" is one such venue that is indeed advocated subliminally by all known theologies. It indeed is the common denominator of every ethos in formation of a healthy community.

From these scriptural translations we find out that in ancient Arabia there was a school of the "Square and the Round." This school of thought advocated the philosophy that the culturally acceptable good was most naturally vested to be round in shape and soft in spirit. They recognized the negatives and drawbacks of the hard-edged elements. They tried to simplify in reality this complex thesis to their community through a visual symbolism. Their reflection was that societal impact of any individual could be compared to natural elements that surrounded us. Elements that are composed of hard edges can be very damaging when they loose their impressive positions and hit the ground not only they cause damage to themselves but to the area of impact.

I used to hear something similar from my sculptor grandfather who would say something like, "that relief contains a lot of hard edged forms, and they need to be softened so they could be more invitational." Did that mean that hard forms are to be rejected? Depending on their degree, yes. As a child you learned that running into hard-edged objects hurt much more than rounded objects.

It is ironic that it took centuries for the economically develop western cultures to begin to use the word "organic" when they tried to express their appreciation of two- and three-dimensional forms that had soft visual engagements in the mid twentieth century as if it was a new discovery by the artists and artisans.

ACHIEVING THE RANKS OF THOSE WITH ROUND HALOS WHILE ON THIS EARTH

Quid fas optare , quid asper
Utile nummus, habet; patriae charisque propinqulus
Quantum elagiri deceat, quem te Dues esse
Jussit et humana qua parte locatus es in re,
Quid sumus, aut quidam, victuri gignimur.

Persius

For what good, is what we aspire
Wealth acquired in such hardship
What is expected of us by humanity?
What was our Creator's demand,
Who are we and what are we the chasers of.

So how does it take for one person to become soft and well-rounded? In the course of the development of the Christian art even those who had achieved sainthood, if still alive, were portrayed with square halos and those who had passed away were depicted with rounded halos. Thusly even the spiritual elders believed that the time we were allocated by our creator

27

was not enough to be totally appreciative of all that is availed to us on this earth by our creator. If we have to deduce anything from the past scriptures and edicts educating our senses does not end by graduating from the most prestigious academic institution or art school. Educating our spirit does not come about simply by going and chanting mantras from a monastery to a mosque.

We have to learn to use the available tools to chisel away, sand and buff the hard edges of our self. It is highly imperative that to be able to achieve a peaceful and productive existence one has to acquire the secrets of self-acceptance. One has to learn to expand the sense of selfhood by learning to include others in one's larger self. We have to concentrate on our potential for self-improvement rather than our present state of imperfection. To get there we have to learn to recognize and thusly affirm what is potentially ours already and forever. It is not very healthy on a long run to spend our energies trying to justify ourselves in eyes "of others." We may be more successful if we do our best by our understanding; then accept the consequences with equanimity.

When we allow the weeds of guilt to grow in the garden of faith we are cultivating within ourselves we diminish the productivity of our culture. It is essential to reflect, knowing that human beings are prone to error; thusly transform all feelings of guilt into a resolution to do constantly better. Neither success nor failure can define one who is made in the image of Infinite Perfection. We were always told that we should mix with those, who in their expansiveness offer support to others; and elude the company of those who are cynical and often insecure.

FINDING THE
RIGHT DOOR TO
CONTENTMENT

The Character Of A Happy Life

How happy is he born or taught
That served not another's will
Whose armor is his honest thought
And simple truth is his utmost skill!

Whose passion not his masters are,
Whose soul is still prepared for death,
United unto the world by care
Of public fame or private breath;

Who envies none that chance doth rise
Nor vice; had ever understood
How deepest wounds are given by praise;
No rules of state, but rules of good:

Who had his life from rumors freed
Whose conscience is his strong retreat;
Whose state can neither flatterers feed,
Nor ruin make oppressors great;

Who god doth late and early pray
More of his grace than gifts to lend;
And entertain the harmless day
With a religious book or friend;

This man is freed from servile bonds
Of hope to rise, or fear to fall;
Lord of himself, thought of lands;
And having nothing, yet hath all.

Sir Henry Wotton

To achieve any goal one has to accept the fact that the hypnosis of self-limitation is breakable. The heights that many have attained can be attained again by others given sufficient time, dedication and properly directed energy by each in his own way. We should recognize that we are each an instrument in the great "Symphony of Life" which is designed to sustain all if one accepts the thesis that it is his responsibility to learn and find the right key to attune himself to its composed harmonies.

HANDICAPPED
BUT, NOT DISABLED

"If one advances confidently in the direction of his dreams, and endeavors to live the life which he has imagined, he will meet with success unexpected in common hours."

Henry David Thoreau, Walden 1854.

"Where there is a will there's a way"

We have faith in old proverbs full surely,
For Wisdom has traced what they tell,
And Truth may be drawn up as purely
From them, as it may from "a well."
Let us question the thinkers and doers,
And hear what they honestly say;
And you will find they believe, like bold wooers,
"Where there's a will there is a way."

The hills have been high for man's mounting,
The woods have been dense for his axe,
The stars have been thick for the counting,
The sands have been deep for his tracks,
The sea has been deep for his diving,
The poles have been broad for his sway,

But bravely he's proved in his striving,
That "Where there's a will there is a way"

Have ye vices that ask a destroyer?
Or passion that needs your control?
Let reason become your employer,
And your body be ruled by your soul.
Fight on, though you bleed in the trial,
Resist with all strength that ye may;
Ye may conquer Sin's host by denial;
For " Where there's a will there is a way"

Have ye poverty's pinching to cope with?
Does Suffering weigh down your might?
Only call up a spirit to hope with.
And dawn may come out of the night.
Oh! Much may be done by defying
The ghosts of Despair and Dismay;
And much may be gained by relying
On "Where there's a will there is a way."

Should you see afar off, that worth winning,
Set out on the journey with trust;
And ne'er heed if your path at beginning
Should be among brambles and dust.
Though it is but by footsteps ye do it,
And hardship may hinder and stay;
Walk with faith and be sure you'll get through it;
For " Where there is a will, there is a way"

Eliza Cook

Way back during my early developmental period of life as an alter boy in church, I heard the priest talking about the prophet Jesus who was preaching in the streets of Jerusalem.

Jesus heard about a man who literally had become a fixture at the main gate of the temple who constantly complained to every passerby about how he was deprived of all life resources; that he had no job, no good food, no good clothes, no friends, no life. Supposedly Jesus walked up to him and listened with great patience. The man who seemed to have mastered all the avenues and techniques of acting is incapable and handicapped. He kept repeating that since it was the Lord's will he deserved and was entitled for gifts and alms in His holly name.

Jesus who had heard enough looked at him with pity and said to him, "Inte kum ene thekhum ma'ak." which means, "You stand up and I will stand up with you."

"Tantum cura potest et ars doloris
Desiit fingere Caleius podagram Martialis"

Caleius

"He so well mastered the art of being handicapped
Deceit finally captured."

The story comes to us from the Roman pundit, Martialis. There was a social parasite, Caleius, who had mastered feeding off and taking advantage of all that was available but avoided being a part of the system. To make the people he benefited from believe that he had a lot of physical problems, wrapped his leg and arms as if defunct and to make sure that he gets utmost attention he patched one eye as if blind. Years later when things changed and felt more comfortable and secure he took of all the theatrical costume of his leg and arm and of course the eye patch. He discovered that he had forgotten how to walk and he sadly found out that his eye he had patched for so long could no longer see.

A friend of mine who was from Konya, a city that served as the base for the Seljuki Empire and home for the world-renowned Dervish Mevlana and his wisdom, recited a stanza of his that affected at least some in class that always had an excuse why they can't. "If you can't leave your space then you could go into yourself, and become a ruby mine, open to the gifts of the sun."

WHAT'S IN THE NAME?

The seeding of artificial entitlement.

The thirteenth-century "Sufi," the philosopher Mevlana, whose wisdom I will share in timely fashion, was so impressive with his knowledge of Greek philosophy that he was coined the name Rumi, which in Arabic meant "The Greek." Even today the western world has difficulty comprehending the ethics of life in remote areas of the Middle East, Central Asia or the Far East that has contributed so much to the cultivation of humanities that even help develop the minds of many western philosophers. The reason I thought that I should mildly touch on this subject that might shed some light on the modus of ethics of identity. It was and still is considered necessary to teach children that they have to earn their proper name that reflects their communal contributions, rather than capitalize on an inherited title. In the contemporary western cultures, the child gets to acquire not only his first name but also the middle and last name, even before his arrival. In past cultures they were lucky if they had one name that was bestowed upon them by the elders as the individual formed a relative identity and character within his community. If he had difficulty achieving any contributive and impacting identity he was simply called as the "son of" or "the father of" so and so of he who has achieved a communal position. As one learned a trade that he could be identified through, then he can earn the name to be recognized by his community for his achievements or that particular talent. The names became Ahmed the Steel Master; Lole the Master Builder; Shoemaker Ali, and so on. The master filmmaker Elia Kazan, who recently passed away, came to this country as Elia with his father's artisan name Kazancian, which meant "the brass potter." Even in the royal aristocracy the children where recognized by their physical, social, cultural, and communal image and granted a title that depicted their identity.

The Emevie warriors of North Africa whose leader, Tarik Bin Ziyad who around the seventh century invaded Spain, his name literally meant "Tarik son of Ziyad." As he crossed the peninsula the mountains were named after him in Arabic Cebel el Tarik; "The Mount of Tarik." Of course centuries later it became "Gibraltar." The Ottoman Emperor Suleyman the Magnificent, (back home his birth name was just Suleyman). Not until he came to power and began to facilitate his subjects with laws that manifested human rights. Thusly he was referred to as "Kanuni Sultan Suleyman" by his subjects. "Kanuni" simply meant "The Law Giver."

Mevlana, the highly recited and quoted Wise Man in all Islamic cultures, his full name was Mevlana Celaleddin Rumi. But he basically started with one name. Mevlana meant that of the "Mevlevi" tribe. But as he traveled and spread the words of wisdom he acquired in the course of his travel he was called "Celaleddin" which meant the "the light of the holly believer." As he eventually ended up in central Asia Minor, today's Turkey, where he greatly contributed to the cultural interaction of the primarily Greek Eastern Mediterranean and primarily Arabic Mesopotamian cultures, he earned the name "Rumi," "The Greek." Well of course many of the European cultures reflect the same mentality. In history we could run into names like the famous Charlemagne, "Charles the Great" had to acquire that title for he was the son of Pepen the Short; Richard the Lion Hearted; Alexander the Great who was the son of Philip the Second; obviously he had little to contribute to earn a respectable title in his homeland, Macedonia, suffering at the time from severe economic mayhem. Maybe that was why Alexander, who was home schooled by no other then Aristotle, advised him that he had to leave his home, to go seek his fortune in far far away lands to acquire that greatness expected from every child by his family.

I bring this subject up because as I mentioned before that in the contemporary western cultures our forbearers select our names long before our birth. We do not have to earn our title that escorts us from birth to burial. Is it possible that this initial mode of entitlement renders some of us handicapped? Many lose their ambition of being a part of a collaborative forum. In the Middle East they told the children that if you have no legs to climb the ladder use your arms God gave you to hold the ladder for someone who needs to get to the roof so he can fix the roof under which you shelter.

God has put a ladder in front of our feet
We all must climb step after step
You have feet
Why pretend to be lame?
You have hands
Why hide the fingers
That can grip

Mevlana Celaleddin Rumi

We, as benefactors of the abundance left by the efforts and sacrifices made by our forbearers, have mastered self-pity.

Victor Kiam

Even if you fall on your face, you're still moving forward.

Drown self-pity in the recognition that emotional self-indulgence only hinders one's ability to accomplish anything Well let's see if a western thinker Goethe, could give us some tips to overcome all artificial hindrances and live a productive life. According to Goethe, there are nine requisites for contented living:

> *"Health enough to make work a pleasure;*
> *Wealth enough to support your needs;*
> *Strength to battle with difficulties and overcome them;*
> *Grace enough to confess your sins and forsake them;*
> *Patience enough to toil until some good is accomplished;*
> *Charity enough to see some good in your neighbor;*
> *Love enough to be useful and helpful to others;*
> *Faith enough to make real the things of God;*
> *Hope enough to remove all anxious fears concerning the*
> *future."*

Johan Wolfgang Von Goethe

The culture within which I was brought up children were thought to believe that those who lacked love, faith, and hope would forever render themselves handicapped. The arts, such as stories, poetry and simple wall carvings always taught us that many of our heroes who were blind, deaf, physically impaired always found avenues to share their hidden God-given gifts with their loved ones. They were appreciated as heroes for centuries to come even if brutally incarcerated on some desolate island by some insecure tyrant.

Having total appreciation of Goethe's mandated requisites for contented living would like to induce only a slight change to his order of needs.

I once heard a teacher of mine mention that prosperity was primarily a state of mind. One has to learn to find the strength in oneself and not wait for the passing waves of circumstances to propel one forward.

I would probably start with "Faith." As indicated before I, like my predecessors would like to begin my day by believing that there is an inherent reason for me being here not just an accident. Thusly like all ready spirits, I can open the curtains of faith so I can put to use all that my creator bestowed in me with respect to warm in spiritual light, rather than darkness.

"Quo timoris minuseat, eo minus ferme periculi est"

Titus-Levius

The less we fear the less in danger

If it is true faith than that could lead to the development of enough "HOPE." With hope one can overcome the fear of the uncertainties of the future. Fear is the most destructive element in one's life that deteriorates the foundations for all other necessary elements in healthy social cohesion. Through hope we need to develop the spiritual strength to nurture patience.

One can only appreciates the importance of "PATIENCE" when some good is accomplished.

To be graceful and loving is basically incorporated when one has developed confidence in his or her inherent possibilities. A person has to be taught that he is only a part of a total. His value is better defined by his graceful interaction with his surrounding elements. Gentle entry into a desired arena has more of a chance of generating the love of acceptance.

"You can give without loving, but you cannot love without giving"

Amy Carmichael

Well, then how does being charitable play a role in contented living? We have a tendency to believe that charity has something to do with wealth. In essence one does not have to be wealthy to be charitable. However while wealth could be an important medium in human facilitation of worldly needs, it is not the means to love, grace and spiritual faith. I recall the elders of my culture telling us that not to discard anything that has served its value for you. Give it to someone and make sure that the receiver feels that he knows you got all you need so it is now his turn to enjoy the benefits. This will teach the receiver that someone else may benefit as well when he is done.

Thusly when any human learns to avail his inner self with, faith, grace, love, patience and hope, then he will have more of a chance at living a truthfully healthy and productive life.

"With weeping you pay no debts; or with curse and laughter."

A Yiddish Proverb

In the era of Sufism in the thirteenth century it was believed that when the external senses were shut off the internal senses, which held the keys to open the doors of the hidden world, had their time.

"He wishes me to get out of myself
He wishes me to sit in freedom.
I was constantly involved with fear and ambition;
He now tells me to break all my chains."

Mevalna Celaleddin Rumi

Sufi of the era most quoted by all cultures and faiths throughout history that lived in the vicinity of Konya, central Turkey that served as the power center for the Seljuki Empire.

Having the privilege of accessibility to many doors with no keys could be as useless as having many keys but no doors. If one is taught early in life to believe that one has more than one door to open so he or she can enjoy the God-given resources, then the debilitating thought of being handicapped will cease to be. But you have the responsibility to cast the key that will fit the door that you want to enter. When called upon, if one does not have the preparedness to open the right door, then one is considered handicapped. If one can educate oneself to believe that one has more than one key somewhere on his neck chain that could open that one door to free himself from all artificial encumbrances. Literally, we can all be considered handicapped if we have not been taught to believe that we are all accessed at least to that one key that can open the gate for the release of our self-identity then entering into the chamber of self-denial.

While in the middle school in central Turkey, a classmate of mine brought a 45 rpm record from America of a famous singer called, Ray Charles. Even though we were in an age of just barely comprehending the English language, we were able to feel deep appreciation of this singer and his expression of his feelings through his vocal intonation. We were able to feel his fears, love and human values even though none of us knew who this singer was. Then one of our American teachers, who taught music, told us the music that we were listening to was created by a black singer who had lost his vision when he was six years old. But he never gave up and never considered himself as handicapped. He was the first musician who was able to blend the pain and suffering of the so-called black jazz with the southern white blue-grass music which none of us had heard of. He went into detail of explaining the intricacies of different musical expressions of different peoples being brought together to be enjoyed and appreciated around the globe by this singer whose memory of visual experience ended at such a young age. But no matter where you go around the world, people of every culture know the name and the universal expression of Ray

Charles. Then who do we consider handicapped? The corporate leader who ripped off his shareholder and disappeared into oblivion with millions without sharing any of his God-given senses or the kid who lost his vision yet can bring love to the doors of those far, far away?

A CULTURE IN FAILURE OF DISTINGUISHING COMEDY FROM TRAGEDY

"Art is a window to eternity."

Plato

"The arts should be the carriers of universal human values for social cohesion but should never be used as weapons for social corrosion."

Sait Giso, my beloved dad.

Life, Liberty, And The Pursuit Of Happiness

Egalite! Liberte! Fraternite

Thomas Jefferson, a member of the wealthy class, as a young man must have learned a lot in the course of his visit to France. His mentor in Paris, no other than, the author of "Poor Richard's Almanac," Good Old Benjamin Franklin, a Royalist, introduced him to the misery of the poor, oppressed, socially disillusioned, hopeless, the very unhappy subjects of the French

43

royal class. It's no wonder that he who had developed the ethics of recognizing the basic human needs inserted the cord for a proper composition of the Declaration of Independence, the globally resonating notes, the rights to "life, liberty and pursuit of happiness."

I was introduced to the "Declaration" by my English teacher, Mrs. Scott, in the first year of my prep school in Turkey at age eleven. She educated us about the wisdom of the founding fathers of the United States, which overseas we all knew as "America." The children in class were very impressed by the historical subject because we all liked to be, free, and pursue a rich happy life. But we were in a country that thought freedom could only be achieved by learning to be a responsible citizen. We could not have access to any of these privileges until we learned to exercise universally acceptable social conduct. Our teachers made sure when we visited archeological museums, went to see a movie or a staged play to see if we observed anything that contained values that we were not aware of.

For us to understand the importance of the privileges extended to us by our parents, family, and community they always took us back into the past to show us how in the course of human history what man could pursue was survival. The arts in every field were no more than messages of what cultures went through just for self-sustenance. Unfortunately today not many have the basic understanding of the inherent meaning of the "Declaration of Independence" especially by the developing young minds that will form the future of this Empire. It is very hard for one to understand the value of these privileges if one is born with and within them. Our developing minds have to be taught that your life is yours and is your private domain. Thusly your liberty and pursuit of happiness should never be exercised by imposing your values and power on others for they have the same human rights. Long before the Declaration there were cultures who preached a similar thesis by reciting, "please Lord forgive us as we forgive those who trespassed into our space of life liberty and pursuit of happiness without invitation."

If Thomas Jefferson was to come back and review today's vast resources of the cultural byproducts the so called human resources, like cinema, literature, and telemedia he would be awed to see the glorification of violence, the shady ethics of the rich and the famous; and especially the most unreal so called reality shows. Pursuit of happiness is not glorifying the rich, and the artificial idols but to have the right for each to travel and seek access to our chosen endeavors with no hindrance due to our race, spiritual, economic or social status; although America has done well in leveling the field for the pursuit envisioned by its' founders. However in the course of time the arts have opened many false artificial and dangerous trails that has availed many dangerous minds the weapon to discredit the true ideology this nation stood for over two centuries.

Entertaining Ethics And The Misuse Of The Arts:

Often I consider myself blessed as an artist to have been born within the residues of the last Empire, the Ottomans that ruled and formulated the lives of many cultures on three continents over seven centuries, and being privileged to be the advocator of cultural humanism in the present Empire, America. However sometimes I feel the corrosive use of the constitutionally availed privileges coded by the founding fathers of my adopted home. I cannot help but think of my prep school in Talas, central Anatolia administered by American academicians. When the teacher in the classroom called on us; the response had to be within the processed academic protocol. I look back and wished that we had the same founders so we could have benefited from the privileges granted by the first and fifth amendments. I always think how much fun it would have been to address the teacher who called upon me to answer the tough question by saying; "Sir I have the right to remain silent and I respectfully decline to respond to the question exercising my constitutional rights that secures me from making an ass out of myself," and gracefully sit down.

The reason I brought this up is primarily related to the destined objectives of the writers of the constitution. I do not believe they ever envisioned that in the future the cultural termites would abuse this privilege of the First Amendment to enter into the cultural air ducts and be the cultivators social pollution.

Samples of arts we are accessed to from the past Greek, Roman and preceding cultures were intended not for just environmental beautification and social entertainment but to establish codes of ethics among the citizens to be a productive participant within the frames of their social contract.

In the old Greek culture we were told that there was a slight difference between comedy and tragedy. As a young boy I was told not to ever forget that if in any event you were the "comic butt" you were the "tragedy." Thusly learning may teach you how not to put yourself into a laughable position.

It is so unfortunate that in my adopted country America, the media is filled with images on talk shows and entertaining courtroom theatricals that are literally saturated with characters who claim to be handicapped and openly benefit from the resources not at all available to the vast majority of the populous around the globe. These characters literally have the chutzpah to volunteer and flaunt in front of millions of media addicts that they have the inherent right to benefit from the resources brought about by hard working citizens and have no obligation whatsoever to contribute in any form or fashion to the culture they suck from.

I am amazed to see social conflicts that have existed for millenniums be resolved within the very serious legal arenas known as courts intended to project social ethics and morality have been turned into an arena of comic circus. The so-called unprivileged have, for the sake of brief recognition, succumbed themselves to be used as stage props. Even the presiding judge is so involved in his or her acting visual image and whose main objective is advancing and maintaining the ratings of the show for self-aggrandizement and undue outrageous self-enrichment must have cheated in the ethics test to act as a legal moderator. It is so tragic that a supposedly logical and ethical trained moderator never asks the characters who seems to be more physically fit than the majority of those living in the third world cultures, why he/she can not and does not put to use other physical and intellectual resources into the system of which he leaches from. Is it possible that these pretentious social moderators themselves are coconspirators in cultural corrosion?

One could easily deduce that when a legal moderator is so concerned in image marketing is suffering from unconscious insecurity. A secure educated and cultivated individual does not have the collective unconscious self-serving agenda by playing a part in a serious arena of justice and turning it into a circus for the uncultivated entertainers and entertained.

As a visual artist and cultural traveler, among all the media exposures I have reviewed, I have found only a couple programs one of which is hosted by a lady to whom I refer to as "Lady O" who selects her subjects that seem to co-relate to her life experiences. The fields that she cultivates with the assistance and support of those who have true experiences in developing fruitful life. That is very admirable to have someone share her life experiences through a universally enjoyable and reflective format. In my opinion this is the type of social member to receive an inter-societal title from the hearts of past and present philosophers and spiritual leaders; for she has earned it.

The other forum hosted and monitored by a gentleman that I refer to as the Southern Sufi, who through humor and anecdotal engagements does direct the disengaged minds to evaluate themselves before they judge others. He does generate a format with many mirrors, which help reflect the true source of their problems being no other but themselves. He does practice the wisdom of the past "Sufis" by directing them to learn not to be the last to recognize their ignorance and ending being the tragic butt.

We are a society blessed to inherit vast economic and cultural resources that could be vested into cultivating universal social ethics and inner aesthetics.

NO ONE POSSESSES THE MAGIC WAND
EXCEPT NASTY M (NATIONAL ASSOCIATION OF SOCIAL TERMITES FOR THE YOUNG MINDS)

A stone carver while working on a project in the demising heat of the day said to his working partner, Heiem, "While I was at the bazaar to buy bread, I saw philosophers carrying their heads in the basket crying aloud, "Wisdom! Wisdom, Wisdom for sale."

Heiem responded, "Yes I keep hearing about them, poor philosophers. They possess this need to sell their heads so they can feed their hearts."

The "telemedia," the most accessible contemporary art form that does not require any training for review, has opened the doors to many self-declared Gurus to market themselves as the holders of all necessary prescriptions nicely packaged especially to all those lost souls. Never in history a culture accessed to such abundance of communicative resources availed to so many have been managed to benefit a select few through subliminal advocacy of collective social ignorance as we are witnessing today.

Ever since the creation of those who have benefited the most from human ignorance have been those gurus who claimed they possessed the power bestowed only upon them by a higher supreme. To avoid being taken advantage of such self-declared ATM healers in the past stories were passed around from village to village by nomadic tribes.

It would almost seem that those who claim the magic wand and take advantage of the privileges granted to them through the airways should annually be recognized and be honored with a "World Golden Septic Award."

AMERICA: LAND OF THE GURUS

Variam semper dant otia mentem.

Lucianus

Disconnected spirit builds fantasy

When Am I Going To Die?

One day a self-claimed local guru walking outside of his village saw a man in a tree trying to chop a branch he was standing on. The Guru yelled at him and told him if he keeps on chopping he will soon fall and seriously hurt himself. The man did not listen and kept on chopping. The guru had not gone too far when he heard a crash. He turned around and the man was on the ground flat on his back. The guru rushed back and helped the man to his feet and walked him back to the village.

The man was so thankful, but managed to get back to the village limping with pain. Everyone he encountered he told about the Guru's prophecy. Everyone told him that he should have listened to him for he is someone who holds the magic powers. After he was healed he went to the Guru and thanked him and said, "Since you knew when I was going to fall you must know and please tell me when I am going to die." The

Guru told him that he can not help him on such heavenly matter that concerns only Allah unless he makes a substantial contribution into the sacred pot of the healers hanging by the door. The villager believing that the Guru had the magic powers he sold most of his sheep put all he had into the much known believer's pot. The man was so vested in his belief of the power of the guru he thought it would be wise to know when he was going to die so he can plan for his proper departure. He continuously went to the Guru's hut begging him to prophesy the finality of his life.

"Please, sir, please tell me when I will die. I know you hold the power." His continuous visitation was becoming very disturbing and highly annoying. To maintain his communal prestige, the Guru had to come up with something highly improbable just to get this moron off his back. When the fellow showed up again the Guru said to him, "Listen carefully. You will die when you hear a mule bray three times from a top of the mount." The villager thanked and gave a bit more of his liquid asset and told him that he will never bother him again.

Only a few weeks later as he was walking up the hill with his brother to go hunting against all mathematical odds; he heard the braying of a mule. Stunned, he listened and sure enough the mule exalted the unfortunate sound the guru had predicted three times. The villager hearing this abhorrent sound with his totally vested belief had a severe heart attack and immediately fell to the ground and died. The brothers carried him to the village and told everyone what had happened. They all knew that his death came about for he was an avid believer of the supernatural power of the guru rather than the universal law of gravity. Thusly, in the Middle East, the saying goes, "You are the guru if you remember never to cut the branch you are standing on." All children are reminded early in life never to abuse the culture that feeds them because it is the branch they are standing on.

EXERCISE
SELF-ACCEPTANCE

"In spite of everything, I still believe that people are good at heart"

Anne Frank

Self-acceptance is found through self-conquest. It is an avenue that can be reached by cessation of hostilities. One can get to the land of self-acceptance by appealing to high principles and avoiding to appeal to people's prejudices in order to win their support. We have to let our feelings be guided by wisdom, proper emotion and selfless love. A good sign of one who has achieved self-acceptance is when one has developed the courage to encourage the strength they see in others but not be a feeder nor cauterize the weaknesses in others. Since like attracts likes, it should be a basic principle to uproot negative expectations from a developing mind and sowing positive ones to eliminate destructive conflicts. Our individual destinies are said to a great extent molded by the expectations we hold of life. Resentment of others is a sign of self-belittlement. We can expand our sense of selfhood by including others in our larger self by viewing their happiness, their fulfillment, and their success as our own.

> *"Today, I will accept the differences between us as part of our beauty together. As a young man the secret of my success is that at an early age I discovered I was not God."*

Oliver Wendell Holmes

The answers we seek for are all stored within us. Stories and proverbs from past times have always played great a role through humorously channeling the self generated insecurities from within. Our social insecurity throughout time has been fed by the false assumption that someone else has got what we are looking for. Is it possible that the seeds of the fruits we are seeking in the neighbor's yard are actually implanted within us awaiting proper cultivation?

THOSE WHO KNOW TELL THOSE WHO DON'T KNOW

The story goes that one-day elders of a small central Anatolian village invited this self-invented wise man to come to their mosque and share some of his wisdom with them. Well after the prayer they walked very eagerly to the courtyard waited to hear the advice and world view of this traveling guru. He slowly walked in from the open gate and slowly and calmly went and stepped on the elevated stool facing the congregation with total command and calmness. Observing the obvious anxiety and eagerness of the crowd, he asked them, "My friends do you know what I m going to talk about?" They all looked at each other in confusion and after a brief pause they all yelled, "Noooo!" Then the wise man said, "Well, if you do not know what I am going to talk about then there is no reason for me to be here!" He gracefully stepped down and without saying a word he left the mosque.

The elders were very disappointed and felt that they offended the holy speaker with their ignorance. So they decided to invite him again and all agreed that if he comes again that they will respond more attentively. So they invited the good old wise man again. He accepted and the following Friday after the prayer he came back and stepped onto the podium and looked around and asked them again, "My fellow camaa' (congregation) do you know what I am going to talk about?" They all looked at him with an agreed upon answer and all in chorus, shouted, "Yesss!" Well the Wiseman stared at them and said, "Well then thank you very much for inviting me. However if you know what I am going to talk about then there is no need to spend your valuable time. Thank you again." He stepped down and left the chamber without saying another word. The elders were all flabbergasted. They did not know what to do. They thought they offended this guru and they had another meeting to see how they can get him back so they can benefit from his wisdom. After a lengthy debate one elder suggested the only alternative, if he accepts the invitation to come, was half the congregation to respond as "yes" and the other as "no." If in case he asks the same question. Thusly he would have no alternative but to share his wisdom. Well, they invited him again and with good grace he accepted to come and address the congregation. They were all eager and ready; looking at him with anticipation of the question. Sure enough the man looked around the hall and asked, "Gentlemen do you know what I am going to talk about?" They were elated and as ready as could be the elders on left side of the hall yelled, "Yesssss!" and the other half from the right side of the chamber all yelled, "Noooo!!!!" They were now very sure they got him this time. Well, he looked around and with a strange smile on his face and said, "I thank you all for being so gracious for inviting me. Having heard your response I know you won't need my wisdom for I will recommend, that those who know, to share what they know with those who do not know." He stepped down and left the chamber.

The philosophers and theologians of the ancient world always believed and preached that the most damaging element in human cohesion is the fear of self-acceptance. When our culture teaches us from the start that everyone no matter how incapacitated has something to contribute. Insecurity is not generated from within. Insecurity can fade away when one realizes that he or she can be contributive if one can recognize the inherent resources within. To learn to be contributive one has to learn to mix with those who, in their expansiveness, offer to support others. One must shun the company of those who, in their contractiveness are cynical or insecure. It is essential not to blame others for their negative attitudes and behavior toward us. For in blaming others we weaken ourselves and thusly give others power over us. If one learns to concentrate on one's potential for self-improvement rather than the state of imperfection one can affirm what is potentially his already and forever. One does not have to try too hard to justify oneself in the eyes of others. All we have to do is do our timely best and accept the consequences with equanimity. One should not allow the weeds of guilt to grow in his garden of faith he is cultivating in himself. We should learn to reflect that human beings are prone to error; they must learn to transform feelings of guilt into resolutions to do constantly better.

LIFE AND KNOWLEDGE

As a town philosopher was passing by a street sweeper in a poor district of Tehran, he looked at the old man and said to him, "If that is all you do in life, I pity you." The street sweeper looked at the passerby and said, "Thank you sir but tell me what is it that you do to earn your daily life?"

The philosopher responded, "I study man's mind, his worldly desires and his deeds." The street sweeper reached for his broom and proceeded with his daily task and with a gentle smile, turned to the philosopher and said, "Sir, I extend a higher pity onto you."

Kahlil Gibran

"The man who has lived the longest is not he who has spent the greatest years, but he who has had the greatest sensibility of life."

Jean Jacques Rousseau

"Youth is a gift of nature, but age is a work of art."

Garson Kanin

The Fruit of wisdom

Wisdom is not to seek avenues just to acquire worldly assets but it is making proper use of what is availed by sharing them with others for healthy and mutual interaction. Thusly the cultivation of the grounds for the seed we want to plant is within us and it is not in a neighbor's yard.

When I was about six or seven years old, I remember a gentleman, who I think was a guest from India named Mr. Kapoor, visiting with my family. As they were enjoying their odorous Turkish coffee, I heard Mr. Kapoor mention something about a heavenly fruit that had something to do with human wisdom. I was very interested. I was wondering if he was talking about the apple Eve gave to Adam. I thought Adam had already eaten it. I came closer to them and asked Mr. Kapoor about this heavenly fruit of wisdom. I asked him where I could get it so I can become as wise and learned as my dad. He smiled and looked at my dad and said, "Well sir, do you think we should tell him?" My father gave him the characteristically Mediterranean affirmative nod with a mildly agreeable smile.

"Well young man," he said, "Yes, there is such a fruit, but I will tell you a story that will give you a clue as to how you can get to it. You see? This fruit is not sold in the fruit bazaar. Just many like you there was a young woman who was very interested in this "Fruit of Wisdom." She traveled all the way to the village of the Dervish, who was known to be not only holy but a wise man. When she met him she was so happy. She asked him where she could get this fruit. The wise man told her that she had to travel and study with him. She wanted to know how long she has to study. When he told her that time was of least importance, she did not think he was as wise as he was portrayed or he really did not know. So, she decided to go on and look for this fruit in other places. She traveled all around the earth searching. She spend thirty years going places, meeting new people with different religions and languages and finally one day she arrived at a garden which was not far from her home. There under this beautiful tree sat the Dervish she had met thirty years ago. He greeted her and with welcoming smile he asked her to look up. As she did she saw this heavenly radiant fruit hanging from the tree. She was so moved but highly confused. She asked the Dervish why did he not tell her that the fruit that she has been looking for all her life was literally in her back yard. The wise man looked at her and said, "If I had told you then, you would not have believed me. In any case even if you had believed me this tree produces this fruit only once every thirty years, and only those who have been seeking it for that many years get to appreciate its real taste."

"Our deeds still travel with us from afar, and what we have been is what makes us what we are."

LIFE AND NATURE

Free and open studio for everyone to learn the proper placement of the self in the Creator's grand composition.

Pumpkins And Walnuts And The Wisdom Of Allah.

Many cultures for centuries have tried to cultivate their youth early in life through humor to recognize the best place where their creator has placed them into the composition. We were told that there was a hidden reason for all elements that surrounded our lives. But we cannot help and still question every aspect of life.

One day a local preacher walked outside of his village and lay down under a walnut tree where he began to look at all the natural beauties that surrounded him. As he looked around he observed this huge pumpkin, which was being nurtured by a small plant, and a huge walnut tree was the nourishing source of this little green fruit, the walnut. He silently found himself questioning the Lord's reasoning for such strange placement. It did not make any sense. He kept thinking about God's unexplainable logic when all of a sudden a walnut fell from the tree on his baldhead. He looked up and thanked Allah that it was not the pumpkin that had fallen on his head from that majestic tree. He looked up into the sky and yelled, "Forgive me, my Allah, for having the audacity to question the wisdom of the placements of life in your composition."

INFORMATION, EDUCATION, CULTURE

"Knowing is not enough; we must apply.
Willing is not enough, we must do"

Goethe

"One must learn by doing the thing; for though you think you
know it, you have no certainty, until you try."

Sophocles c. 469 -406 B.C. Greek
tragic playwright Trachinia

He Is A Thinker

One day an old man was walking around in a bazaar in ancient
Jerusalem. He noticed a colorful bird fetched ten pieces of gold.
He walked to them and asked why anyone would pay so much
for a bird. The bystanders said to him that the bird was a very
rare breed that in the north they were called "parrot" and he
can talk. The old man immediately went to his home and came
back with his pet turkey. He said that his turkey was worth at
least one hundred pieces of gold. They looked at each other in
awe and asked him why he thought that this ordinary bird is

worth that much. His answer, "Gentleman that bird that was sold for ten gold pieces could talk but this bird thinks."

Let me start with one of my encounters with basic principles of life. It was my first year at a prep school that you will probably hear more about. I was assigned a seat in the dining hall, which was referred to as table five. My seat faced the wall. Right above the shoulder of the table prefect, the senior in charge of table etiquette and mannerism hung a sign. It was in English. Since all at that table were prep class kids, I recall none of us had command of the basics in this language. That's why we were there; to learn this new language that not many spoke. For some reason, maybe it was because that nicely framed sign was always facing me I crudely memorized it without knowing what in the world it said. The writing on the wall read:

INSTRUCTION ENDS IN THE CLASSROOM
BUT EDUCATION ENDS ONLY WITH LIFE

Only years later, even though I had a good command of the English language, I comprehended the true meaning of that little framed saying hung ten feet away from my feeding domain table five, for nine months. It made sense that education facilitates us with the necessary elements stored in the social warehouse that enable us to properly polish the mirror of the inner spirit to reach the true self. I will try to share with you some stories about my life encounters that taught me love, passion and patience that made the path to spiritual growth.

I am now at a point in my life where I feel obligated to start with basic definitions of some highly misused expressions in western society. Unfortunately, not only have we made it a habit to misuse such words as education, information and culture, through the availability of mass media, we do a tremendous disservice by imposing them on the so-called developing societies. Let me explain.

Let us take the loosely used word, "information." One would hear something like, "That guy is really educated. He has a doctorate from one of the top ten Ivy League colleges." Being highly informed does not really mean that one is equally educated. And being highly educated does not make one equally cultured.

"Education should be the process of helping everyone to discover his uniqueness"

Leo Buscaglia

There is a story of two laborers. Two men were working very hard; one was swinging his heavy pick into the ground while the other was shoveling away. It was a very hot day. At one point one of them stopped and told the other to take a few minutes to ask him something. "What is it?" he asked. "You know I have been wondering. All my life I have been a worker and have been in every town in the country and met so many people, learned to share the good and the bad. I have learned so much about the needs of life from the rich, the poor, from all those who have been there, but have never been to school." "So?" the other mumbled. "You know, my greatest wish is to have enough money and go to school to be a professor, and if I am lucky one day to have the opportunity to share all I have gathered with those who really deserve to know about real life." Looking into the sweaty face of his coworker, he asked, "What would you wish to do if you had the resources?" The other man who has been patiently listening uttered, "I had all the resources and I was a professor, but hell, I have been nowhere, done nothing and never had a life."

One's social connectivity cannot be defined or measured by the amount of data he has registered within the cranial warehouse. In fact it is very important to be informed. However, the information deposited can begin to display its value only when put to use. As one begins to activate the data one begins to realize there are more than one way to make use of that data. When the dry and inert information begins to be a part of the sensory process and one learns how to properly respond to givens, then the process of education leads the educated senses into the third phase "culture."

"Vinegar is the end of the failed wine; its best hiding place, "salad."

Sait Giso, my dad

A simple example I could compare it to would be, the basic fundamentals of making of good wine. You may have all the data to make wine, for selecting the right grape, the proper format of juicing, the right container, proper storage temperature; and all the necessary data from the wine connoisseur. Guess what? With all that collaborative input one still has to wait until all that concoction has the needed time to be cultured. If you want to make use of what you put together earlier than the inherent processing time then what you end up with is nothing but vinegar.

Unfortunately that's why we have a society filled with PhDs who can only exercise their validity in a bowl of intellectually tossed academic salad. It is essential that our teachers learn to teach proper processing rather then storing and recycling the information they release onto their students.

Information that sleeps idly has been the subject matter for many artists in every dimension because a true artist has to know that any information that has not been experienced by any of our situated senses does little or no good to the acquirer, to the receiver, or to humanity.

Information acquired through others is never as potent and cultivating as the one acquired by vested engagement in that

social experience. It may help a bit if we walk in Ben Johnson's
shoes through his ode to himself;

Where dost thou careless lie,
buried in ease and sloth?
Knowledge that sleeps doth die;
And this security,
It is the common moth,
That eats on wits and arts, and destroys them both.
Are all the Anonian springs
Dried up? Lies Thespia waste?
That now a nymph now sings?
Or droop they, as disgraced,
To see their seats and bowers by cahtt' ring pies defaced?
If hence thy silence be,
As 'tis too just a cause,
Let this thought quicken thee:

Minds that are great and free
Should not on fortune pause;
This crown enough to virtue still, her own applause.

What through the greedy fry
Be taken with false baits
Of worded balladry,
And think it poesy?
They die with their conceits,
And only piteous scorn upon their folly waits.

Then take in hand by lyre,
Strike in thy proper strain;
With Jephets's line aspire
Sol's chariot for new fire.

To give the world again;
Who aided him will thee, the issue of Jove's brain.

And since our dainty age
Can not endure reproof,
Make not thyself a page
To that stumpet, the stage;
But sing high and aloof,
Safe from the wolf's black jaw and the dull
ass's hoof.

Ben Johnson

One day as I walked into a popular bookstore in Chicago, I was struck by the number of books published and literally designed for color, form and texture for the fast-food consumer as fast recipe for the idiots who missed the boat of cultural humanist interaction.

One can only know by being where the doing is done. Yes, Plato's theory of "anamnesis" that we are born with some sense of inherent knowledge, but many ancient thinkers suggest that we may be here to relive so we can appreciate what we did not in the past.

So how do we do that?

Is there a recipe?

WHO HAS GOT THE RECIPE?

Not anyone I know.

Emperor Dionysus used to have great pleasure mocking the linguistic scholars of his time and would examine and debate the misfortunes and spiritual depressions of Odysseus by comparing them to the musicians who expertly knew how to tune their instruments but failed to fine tune their life and the scholars who preached of social justice but failed to practice it in their daily lives.

Many I run into, claim they just got the answer and the recipe to a situation that has been bothering them for a long time. I remember, when I was ten or eleven years old, thinking I was cool because I was reading all these famous thinkers' books that I heard the elders discuss in the course of social occasions. My cousin, Burhan, who was two and a half months older then I, caught on to the idea that if we were really going to be somebody like our parents, we better read these heavy authors. We went to a section of town where they sold discards of every kind and found used books, with torn covers and missing pages by, Montaigne, Daniel De Foe, Marx. We had heard the names from the elders but we were not of age to be properly introduced to them. It was an era where the word "communism" was a topic talked about behind closed doors. We did not know what it was. We knew from hearsay that this German guy called Marx had something to do with it. So, Burhan and I chipped in a quarter of a lira and bought a, parts-missing book and tried to read it to the best of our capacity. We both knew if we read important stuff we could be part of the important circle and more acceptable by the elders. Well, we read and tried to find things that were of importance with our limited comprehension. We found parts that were very acceptable to two eight-year-olds. Especially appealing were the points that related to equal right and equal distribution of wealth. Nowhere did it mention about the conditional dispersement of allowance to all the mandated chores. Wow! This was fantastic. We both decided to go home and convince our parents to look into this thing called "communism." We believed if we convinced them to this ideology, we would have equal say and rights at home. We would not have to wait for the measly lire weekly allowance; a big chunk of which we had to dispense on Sundays to the collection tray in church. We would have equal distribution of that wealth. This was good. We had to do nothing according to Marx that we totally agreed with and we had equal rights and privileges.

That evening after dinner, I asked my dad if I could talk to him about something very important that I wanted to share with him. He invited me to his reading chamber. He asked me what it was all about. I began to tell him about the importance of this new worldly recognized thinker and his very important ideas. As I was trying to educate him about communism and try to make it as simple as possible so he might look into it. To my surprise his visual gestures were indicating positive and gentle conformity. From my past experiences with him, I felt something was awfully fishy. He softly said, "This is really nice. I am so glad you brought it to my attention. Your mom and I should really look into this. I am very impressed. Oh, by the way before I forget, I meant to compliment you for the new suit you got from the tailor. English wool is it?" "Yes," I said. "Beautiful cut, I must say." How much did you pay for it?" "I don't know, mom took care of it," I politely uttered, with a smile that I was quite familiar with. "The shoes," he remarked, "very elegant and they go nicely with that suit. I really like them. You have good and quite expensive taste. How much did you pay for them?" I said, "Dad, you bought them, you should know." I knew something was not right. Here this man, a community leader, has difficulty staying on course so I could give him some tips on this idea of communism. "By the way," he said, "do you like living in this house? It's a nice place. Is it not?" I was beginning to get irritated. Then I realized as usual he was up to something. I knew immediately where he was heading when he asked me if I was paying any rent to live there. He looked at me with a well-rounded and professorial smile and said, "Son, with all these benefits and not very clear job description you are the ideal communist." I looked at him and not knowing why I gave him my collaborative affirmative smile and headed to the door. As I was about to exit, he said, "By the way, tell your cousin that not only are you a communist, you are a rich communist." I went out thinking that my cousin and had done it again. We did not study the matter long enough not to make Asses of ourselves. However, as I look back, I appreciate the fact that at that age we had the guts to try to put to test and see all that sophisticated ideas advocated by leading adults would really work to benefit two eight year olds.

As I mentioned earlier, everyone on this planet is searching for answers even for the simplest human situations through accumulating tons of data acquired through millions of hours of research in laboratories, testing centers, academic forums, and millions of research institutions and foundations. When I take a chance to participate in some of these engagements just to make sure that I exercise the open-door policy that I stand for, I come out thinking of the simple story told to kids in Turkey about the local Hoca (the Islamic priest) the famous Nasreddin Hoca.

One day, Omar the village Molla, "intellectual" in the mountains of Turkistan, walked from his place out in the country all the way to the village bazaar. While shopping he ran into a couple of friends who told him that they just got this fantastic recipe for liver "kebob." He thanked them and bought a loaf of bread and lamb's liver. That was all he could afford. For him this was a treat. He began to walk back to his home. He was way out in the open prairie. Beginning to feel the hot sun and the distance he still had to walk he decided to pray and thank Allah that he gave him all this wisdom and gift to explain things to others who were not blessed with the intelligence that was bestowed upon him. He felt good about everything and began to think about the treat he was carrying and as he began to chant "Allah u Auqbaur" "God is greatest," as an eagle appeared in the sky. As he was looking up and observing this fast flying creature above him, he was surprised and got caught off guard as the eagle dove with swiftness towards him and picked the liver out of his hand and flew away.

He could not believe what was happening. He knew he could do absolutely nothing to get his special treat back and in his frustrated anger he shouted, "You idiot, you took the liver but guess what, I have got the recipe right here, the recipe. I have the recipe, you idiot, you hear me the recipe."

Now you tell me who is the idiot? The eagle who enjoyed the food or the intellectual who has the recipe?

NO THERAPY NEEDED
IF YOU REALIZE SNOW
WILL EVENTUALLY MELT

Nam verae voces tum demun pectore ab imo
Ejiciuntur, et erpitur persona, manet res.

It is when words uttered from the heart
The mask will drop and true face will stand.

In the Middle East the saying goes, "The snow will eventually melt and then we shall see where the dog has made his mess." Which literally means that if you have done anything that you think is not socially acceptable do not hide it. The sooner you come and face it, the sooner you will be able to deal with the consequences. With all the communal resources that are availed to us if we simply are taught early in life that no one is perfect. We all make mistakes. Even when we read about the unjustifiable behaviors and deeds in the stories related through the Holy Scriptures starting with Adam and Eve. Can you imagine Adam denying his behavior, by responding to the Creator about the missing apple, "I don't know who ate it, God, ask Eve." How about Eve saying, "Dear Lord we were just sitting there and the apple just fell into Adam's mouth as he was looking up at your throne praying. I swear I did not give it to him."

We know not only God knows what happened up there but it would be a fair assumption that both knew the rules but failed to adhere to them. This fear of being ejected from the format that we desire to be within so we master the techniques of hiding the truth. One day as a child, I heard an Arab lady, whom I as a child loved for her humor and honesty, say to her husband who was trying to portray his image in question, "Darling, you do not have to tell me who you really are for I have seen you under the sheets and over the sheets." Later on in life when I began to be a bit more sophisticated, I found out that it was an Arabic saying commonly used in the Middle East to confront those who suffered from communal insecurity due to the fact that they camouflaged so much of their true identity.

PLEASE COME IN.
MEET YOURSELF!

"Do not break the mirror if you hate the image you see"

A proverb.

When you enter into the chamber of human encounters be aware that you can only get a better reflection of who you are if you do not force the reflectors to give you false images of yourself. I heard once, one of my teachers told me that all people you meet in life are merely mirrors of you. You cannot love or hate something about another person unless it reflects to you something you love or hate about yourself.

In the course of my travels, no matter where I am because of the availability of mass media, I hear the same universal tune over and over again. With all the available resources how we have managed to create the most disconnected atmosphere that ever existed in the history of mankind; not even in the Greek mythos of Echo the beauty that uttered the last sound and Narcissus who was in love with himself.

Today Narcissus and Echo have become one. We are literally surrounded by a multitude of empty spirits who not only are in love with their undefined and highly obscure self, and like to exude the power of the last say for self-assurance social relevance. Thusly they fail to put themselves in the other person's shoes. They could contribute more by learning to consider the other's point of view, and decide whether or not they should refer to it before marketing their own.

To those who have the misfortune of entering the domain of those Echo-Narcissus organic sculptures just remember the secret of self-acceptance is always to bear in mind that the ultimate judge of your social impetus resides forever within yourself.

DISCONNECTED SOULS

Nowadays everyone you run into tries to come across as a philosopher. When I go to the local café for a cappuccino, I run into a lot of people who are sitting alone at a table for four and reading the latest report of how to deal with all the social negations that are affecting us. Sometimes I fantasize while I am with a group that is composed of individuals who have never been anywhere, have never experienced any dire circumstances, yet are highly rich in opinion to have as we exercise free fascination of a few archaic philosophers theologians like Moses, Abraham, Jesus, Mohammed, Buddha, Plato, Epictetus, Tukydides, Aristophanes, Sophocles, just walk in and sit with them. I bet they would have a blast.

I have never encountered anyone who has not read the latest book that has all the up to date remedies to all the problems. Why we are not healthy, creative, rich and happy. They all claim to have all the answers. When I encounter them again I see nothing has changed. The same old melody exists, another rondo.

One of my dear and most admired multilingual, highly educated friends who had a position in a newly founded college, with old Oxfordian principles, shared with me some of his bizarre observations. He told me that God has sent him to the garden of intellectual parody. He told me that at this academic institution the professor who taught psychology was twice divorced, on antidepressant medications and with several

DUI citations. The professor who taught art could not draw. The professor who taught physical education was physically unfit, due to highly gravity contesting weight he could barely carry around and the professor who was teaching business was always broke. Almost every month a few days before payday, this person he barely knew would go to his studio and ask if he could borrow some money from him. One day he told me that he came to his office to ask if I could help him out. He asked him to sit down and share with him a bit about how he got to where he is now. All he knew was he was a professor but did not know exactly what he taught. In the course of their dialogue he related to him about the fantastic institutions he attended and the sophisticated education processes he had gone through to land this position to teach Basic Principles of Business Resource Management. He told me that he looked directly into his eyes and said to him; "Listen, as an artist, who in our society is considered lowest on the socio-economic pole? Dr. X, if your best student follows the principles of the basic economics that you advocate and put to practice all the sophisticated theories, I have a feeling that he would be broke and have to borrow quite frequently, just to make things work. The bad part is he will be borrowing from an artist." Well, he told me that he never saw the professor of macroeconomics again. However, I heard now that educator was promoted to serve as the Dean of the Business and Economic Department

I have had the privilege to live among the peoples of many nations and cultures. One fascinating common connection is the universality of human behavior. Having been born and exercised my childhood life and its basic values in an ancient city seated on the rocky cliffs overlooking the Tigris River, now called Diyarbakir, I did not then, but now looking back I consider myself very blessed to witness the most colorful weave of cultures of Assyria, Caledonia, Armenia, Persia, Arabia, Turkic of many preserved and multi-theosophical sub ethos, within the walls of this ancient, rarely-mentioned historical land and cradle of faiths.

Let me tell you. To be able to have a life in the midst of this most engaging format, one had to learn early in life how to properly respond to the needs of others before oneself. One most educating form of communication was to understand parables. I am saying this because our elders, who acted as the educators of our senses, always tried to engage us to the sensible life processes through telling us a little story or funny anecdote that related to whatever it was that bothered us. It taught the young how to fit the format without becoming a "comic butt."

No matter what historic background you had in this ancient city you had to very fast develop the reflex for proper universal response to every occasion.

One of the most important lessons was to know the full value of what one is delivering and its impact on what is already there. Like a painting any element placed on a canvass has the responsibility to add to the meaning of the total composition. In the Middle East it is known as "Knowing one's place." The English call it "fitting." What does it require to properly fit, to supplement and compliment the space one demands?

If it was to be expressed through a scientific axiom one could easily say that one's output cannot surpass one's total input. Thusly one does not have to have a doctorate in social ethics to demand more then his total contribution. Ironically everyone on this planet has something to contribute to the composition they want to be a part of but knowing where, when, and how to place their gift.

WHAT ARE YOU DELIVERING?

I was born in a house very close to a an open field the Turks called "Gavur Meydani" which meant "Valley of the Infidel," a domain of highly preserved Caledonian/ Assyrian Christian ethos that survived through millennium the reigns of Assyrian, Roman, Seljuki, and the Ottoman Empires. The house was assumed to have been built back during the early Ottoman era with a huge courtyard. Three Christian families of different ethnic backgrounds shared a Turkish bath and a fountain within the high wall of this structure. Thusly all sharing Turkish as a common language and three other languages were spoken among the members of each family. So if a child wanted to play with the neighbor's kid, who is in essence confined to the courtyard for most of his playtime, had to learn the other's home language. It did not make any difference of how poor the accent and mode of delivery. There was no other way out if one had to play with the other. Since the parents spent most of their time for social and economic preservation the children had to learn how to get along with each other since that was all that they had.

Since I was the youngest of the crew of the enclosed courtyard, I did not benefit from the privileges often extended to those who were of school age and had an arena where they could have more fun. I had heard so much about this place called "School." To me it meant I had to wait two more years to enjoy the benefits extended to my courtyard mates. Well, what was I to do? The exit to the street from the courtyard was a huge Roman door. I had made several attempts to try to lift the huge iron latches so I could get to the street so I could play with others who had acquired street privileges, with no success. However I had learned that if I acted with a certain manner, which my mom could not tolerate, she would write a note and tell me to take and deliver it to the elders in my grandmother's house. This was a bigger house on the same street only a block away. I loved it.

I was momentarily free and all I had to do was just deliver this note. However since I did not know how to read I, for a long time, did not know what the note said. But I did the job anyway. When I reached my grandma's house, since I could not reach the beautifully crafted bronze knocker, I had to find a hand-size rock on the street and pound on this huge arched door. Well, when someone in the house opened the door, I handed the note and thinking that I have done what I was sent for I wanted to leave so I could go find someone to play with. But, No!!! For some reason, whoever I handed the note to, always managed to get me in and close the door. Now I was confined in another courtyard. Only years later I found out the note I delivered to my grandma's house simply said, "Take this boy and keep him". Now I tell this story to those who ask me why I speak so many languages. I tell them because I never want to deliver my own arrest and detention warrant ever again. I want to make sure that I know what it is that I am delivering.

I was not aware that I had not yet acquired the sense to realize the package "me" that I was delivering was not yet ready for prime-time social engagement. In a nutshell I was a social element in training with limited market value.

BE READY TO SWALLOW
WHAT YOU CAN'T SELL

The Despot and his Tax Collector

One day Hoca Nasreddin happened to be present in the court of the vicious Asian Timurlane as the tax collector was presenting his receipts of the taxes on endless parchments. He kept coming out with piles of accounting sheets that did not seem to be very convincing to the heartless ruler. "Is this all you have collected?" he asked with a very disturbed motion. Having the collector being aware of the falsely-generated rumors of his embezzlement and cheating practices might have reached the Despot's ear, he responded, "Your highness I work very hard to collect all that your subjects owe you and duly record every "akce" I collect, so respectfully I decline to swallow all the fabricated lies about my cooked books to your highness."

Timurlane looked at him and then he said, "Well, in that case you can start right now." The Collector, confused, looked up at his master and asked, "Start what, Sire?"

Timurlane said, "Start swallowing all that you have cooked that you expect me to swallow as proper documentation of all collections you are presenting me with." The collector, highly familiar with his master's ferocity and detrimental possible alternatives, began stuffing one parchment after another into his mouth and kept on swallowing till he was so stuffed that he fell to the ground and passed out. Timurlane thusly turned to Hoca Nasreddin and told him that he was assigning him to the post of general collector.

The Hoca realizing the demanding and scary situation he was put in had to come up with a solution to avoid his predecessor's destiny. He went home and told his wife about his dire situation. For weeks he thought about how to deal with the twisted mind of his master. One day, as he entered his home pondering about the dire position he observed his wife who was preparing Turkish "yufka" a very thin rolled out fresh dough customarily served with cheese and cold cuts. He realized he had the solution for his problem. He asked his wife to roll as many of these thin sheets of dough as she can. He began recording all the collections and proceeds on these "yufka" sheets. When at the end of the month the time of reporting came, the Hoca loaded all his recorded pastry sheets and all the bags of collected tax revenues on his mule-cart and went to the Court of his master Timurlane.

The palace guards helped carry the bags to the seat of the master and placed them at his feet. The master, pleased with the bags of collections, demanded to see the documentation of the collections and thusly asked the Hoca for the records. The wise Hoca pushed the cart piled with the pastry sheets. Timurlane asked the Hoca, "What in the world are these supposed to be?" "The accounting documentation, Sire." "Why are they recorded on these "yufkas?" The wise Nasreddin replied, "Only one of us may have to swallow the bookings of my labor, Sire!"

In old Mesopotamian cultures, long before the biblical era, the people always taught their children to be honest of what they have put into the cooking pot for eventually they will be the ones to end up eating what they have cooked.

WHAT IS YOUR WORTH?

My grandmother's house, even though much larger and more spacious than ours, felt more confining because there were no children even after school. Now I had no one to play with. Obviously this affected my behavior. In the middle of the courtyard was a pomegranate tree. It had the most colorful flowers and eventually it bore a most tasty fruit. The problem was that I was too little to climb it. So I would throw my wood-bottom sandals, the Turks called them "takunya," to see if I could hit one of the fruits. I was told not to do that but what was I to do. So when I felt it was the right time I would make several attempts to knock one of these down. Often I missed. Sometimes I was lucky. But often I was not.

Now here is the best part. My grandfather, a highly-admired master sculptor who had breathing difficulties, was often told by his doctor to control his smoking habit. He was constantly coughing and keeping everyone up all night long. So my grandma would allow him maximum six cigarettes before he left to his work site. When I had reached an intolerable level of behavior my grandma would tell my grandpa that she will allow him to have two extra cigarettes if he takes me with him. Imagine! I am standing there; in my presence, my grandma would say, "two extra cigarettes if you take him with you." I will hear my grandfather say, "No! Him?" I would not even consider taking him for less then ten cigarettes." Now I turn and look at my grandma and she will say, "four." He would say, "eight and not one less." She would say, "Five and that's it." And he would respond, "All right! All right! I'll get him off your hands." At that age, I observed my actual market value was five cigarettes.

Even at that age, I looked for ways to make maximum use of this stage of life, which exercised no inherent rights. Early on I sensed the great possibility of a payback, thusly I did not mind. Going to the work site was more engaging than the confined courtyard. Here I realized that my grandpa was a very important man. His apprentices treated me like a prince. I was allowed to play with all the sculpture tools and chisel on pieces of rocks as if I were one of them. Without knowing I was already an involuntary inducted apprentice absorbing all the basic principles necessary for the bachelor of fine arts at the age of five and a half.

My sister Verjen and my brother Jak, who were four and two-and-a-half years respectively older then me, had the privilege of being treated very special for they had to be prepared to go to this place called school. They were fed, dressed, groomed, and escorted to the door to walk to the school with their neighboring buddies. Me, I was in protective custody with utmost social scrutiny. Are we talking about a second-class citizen? "No." How about a no-class resident?

Once, while playing in a neighbor's courtyard, I heard from some of the kids some ridiculous story that in a place called America they had a thing called "Play School." You could not beat that. Where we lived we did not have that fantastic idea. Well in our culture, children above the age of six everyday around four o'clock came home in their black and white uniforms. They always talked about what they learned that day. I had had it.

After two years of this life of courtyard confinement finally my sister told me that pretty soon I would be able to join them in this fantastic place called school. When the time came I found out I was two-and-a-half months short of the required age for entry. Thank God we lived in a place where rules could be gracefully bent if the cause was for the general welfare and passed the approval of the elders. My father happened to know the town mayor and the school principle. They agreed to overlook this simple matter of minimum age requirement; I was thusly a member of the royal club, school to enjoying the daily release from the family elders' commanding domain.

Actually everybody was happy, my mom, my dad, and all the members of grandpa's elite courtyard cabinet. Well, I was ecstatic to wear my school uniform and go to this place I have fantasized about all this time as a haven of freedom and play. Yeah-right! I will never forget my first morning ordered to learn the military like regimentation. All the classes lined up in ranks. We had to stand in total harmony and coordination to sing the national anthem, which was followed by the pledge of allegiance, which I had no idea what I was reciting with the student assembly. My sister and my brother tried at home to teach me to recite the words properly and with correct Turkish diction so my classmates won't think I am one of those infidels. Not only did I have to learn how to read and write with the proper grammar, but also I had to develop the qualities so I can help my classmates. If they learned something from me then they will be better friends. Even though at that age I did not know much about the importance of the right national class identification I was made to learn reciting the national anthem and the Turkish pledge of allegiance every morning lined up facing the flag. I was barely six years old and I did not know exactly what it was I was reciting. But for some reason it made me feel important and a part of this new allegiance I had inadvertently joined. Ironically having not yet achieved the ranks of those with total comprehension of the recital yet the ending of the pledge, which impressed me the most and went like this:

Yasam
Buyuklerimi saymak ve
Kucuklerimi korumaktir
Varligim Turk Varligina
Armagan olsun

My pledge
Respect to my elders
Protect my youngers
May my existence be pledged to
Turkish existence.

If I had the privilege of being present during the composition of this pledge I would have recommended that the composer change the last line to;

"I pledge to enhance all, wherever I may be.
With my being be pledged to humanity"

"And with the bill of rights
To help me with this new
Phase of imposed conformity."

The two simple lines of the pledge however that was most influential on these young minds were, "I will respect my elders and protect my youngers." That put everyone in a contractual position of acquisition of respect by the strong could only be achieved by display of responsibility by helping and protecting the weak.

At that young age, I liked it. This created a bond between myself and my classmates.

All my expectations however it did not turn out to be what I had envisioned. Yes, we played; but the classes we had to attend and the learning we had to do was not part of what I had imagined school was supposed to be. On top of it we have to get good grades. In Turkish the word grade sounded harsher when they used the word "broken number" for a failing grade. So when we heard the teacher say, "My son if you do not want to get a broken number (failing grade) you better shape up." Obviously my proper attention made my classmates and teachers consider me as a very responsible, studious and attentive boy. In the classroom we did not have separate desks as many modern schools. Three kids shared a desk and a bench. I realized a while later that the child seated in the center was one who could get along and was willing to share resources with the kids on either side.

I sat between a girl on my left and a boy on my right. One day, during recess, the boy I shared a bench with, Haaiem told me he was Jewish and the girl on my left Emel was Turkish Muslim. I did not know what these religions meant. We were like brothers and sister. Haaiem lived very close to where we lived. He was not very good in arithmetic; but he was very nice and giving. I used to help him after class and even during class I would let him peek at my paper so the teacher won't detain him in class for extra study while we were engaged with courtyard privileges during recess. His family used to sell school materials so he would always bring me a free pencil. Emel on the other hand was very alert, smart and pretty. She however, sought my help in the drawing class. I really loved them and loved the atmosphere because we three felt like we were brothers and sister. Here I realized the value of subordinating my needs to the needs of others generated a fulfillment in friendship I learned happiness was kindness, and seeing others as extension of myself.

CREATIVITY

Avenue For Proper Channeling Of Inner Emotions: Self-Expression

Who can claim living a good life
Without music, poetry and art?
Who can attest to a vision of social conscious
Without a gentle and symphonic heart?

Time has been man's best friend
By sharing memories of past, with no end.

Reminding us all
To avoid the power holders
And of those Inferior t'all

Whose belief that knowledge
Is a venue for grieving
As for hope
A device of self-deceiving

And of love and passion
Only be exalted with ration
And in every social inning
Used as devices for pinning

Seek a teacher
Who has been there
And can show you how
To light the candle
So you can see
And with all to share

Beauties of the earth
And that of heaven
In the chamber of hope
With love and passion.

Ano

It is most essential in the process of our upbringing we are taught to learn to receive and properly respond to the needs and inner feelings of others so our feelings and values can be received, processed and appreciated. Proper release of bottled feelings and emotions is most essential in eliminating fear of social acceptance.

Human expressions do not have to be offensive to attract response. In my opinion offensive behavior is the by-product of failed proper emotional release. Thusly the arts avail us with the arena filled with all forms of modes of expressions to release our spiritual and worldly feelings elegantly. If this release is not gracefully shared as history has demonstrated time and time again humanity has taken the whip.

INDUCED CREATIVITY

It is highly essential that one learn early in life to distinguish between creativity and camouflaged duplicity. Creativity is a first person act. One can never give birth to someone else's baby. In the West children are encouraged to be creative but guess what? The child is encouraged and induced just to fill in the preprocessed artificial format. A teacher walks into a so-called art class where every child is equipped with a set of crayons of every color imaginable and a coloring book. Imagine, the visual forms the child is seeking are already defined by someone who has no idea of the meaning of art. Then the teacher asks the children to begin to color. Now how does one expect to have the child who is being taught not to go beyond the predefined line but just fill in the blanks to be expressive. The medium used can not be mixed to the taste and sense of that particular child either. Then years later in college you see students with an abundance of materials and preprocessed techniques try to exercise creativity. What they end up with is nothing more then preapproved and expected redundancy. It cannot happen. Creativity has given way to reproduction and often gracefully hidden emptiness.

Here is the most important avenue available to all. Through proper channeling one can share ones feelings, emotions, values, through the most acceptable format, which we generally call artistic expression. What do we do? We forfeit this privilege of proper portrayal of our identity by singing the tune that is the most marketable.

One must not wonder why artists for reason of recognition and success find it secure to belong to a school of thought that is à la mode. Mode of delivery, not the content of the expression, is the subject most emphasized by moronic intellectuals.

If one has not gone through and has not experienced the true realities of life, then one should not present insight and wisdom. As once T.S. Eliot expressed his observation by saying; "That those who pine up for philosophy in this ampler sense, logical positivism is the most conspicuous object of censure. It is certain that logical positivism is not a very nourishing diet for more then the small minority that has been conditioned to it. When the time of its exhaustion arrives, it will probably appear in retrospect, to have been for our age the counterpart, of surrealism: for as surrealism seems to provide a method of producing works of art without imagination so logical positivism seems to provide a method of philosophizing without insight and wisdom."

Indeed, I find it very humorous when even art historians make so much out of nothingness just to make their observations acceptable and authoritative by categorizing the mode of the expressions and certain trends of times. Nobody seems to ask certain and logical questions. What real artist does any work without expressing himself? That's for the so-called Expressionists. What real artist, who no matter what subject of real interest to him, does not slide into his work a part of all of his impressions? That's for the Impressionist. What real artist puts more emphasis on materials and technique of delivery rather than the content of his subject. Could we say that an Abstract Expressionist could be someone who is trying to express a serious concept but chooses to be intentionally vague? Could we rightfully conclude the artist either does not have total command of his subject matter or intentionally for some unexplained reason chooses to be vague just to elude the subject?

This is like going to a media embellished restaurant and order something on the menu to eat. What was served not only tastes bad but turns out to be indigestible by those who had the stomach to bear this "assemblage" concoction. However, when you ask the host what the hell that was. His answer, "My impression sir is that our new chef puts more emphasis on expressing himself than feeding you."

It is a reporter's task to report the unedited facts, provided he has access to them. It is the artist's task to express his feelings and impressions of his private experiences. In the court of human aesthetics it is not valued to express someone else's spiritual encounters. That came very close to just being a messenger to someone else's spirit.

My experience has been that creativity generally is not triggered by high accessibility. In fact I could venture to say abundance and accessibility deteriorates creativity. Senses go to work when there is need. The well-trained senses make maximum use of available resources.

The format of the creative engagement during my childhood was unique. Imagine very few in the classroom had what we call "a set" of this or that related to materials. The most a kid may have, no matter what economic background, were an ordinary pencil and maybe a couple of colored pencils used by an older brother or sister. If you had three or four, were you somebody? Not at all. You were somebody if you had some elements that were not purchasable but self-developed. Thusly, very early in life you were taught that the value was not in the resources but in the proper and creative use of them.

The best way to learn how to express and share imaginative understanding of the read and heard words went something like this. The teacher would read a story and then she would say, "okay, children now you draw the story you just heard. Draw the part that you liked and that impressed you the most."

I will never forget. The first story was from the Gilgamesh, old Asian stories we were told. The part that really affected me the most was the hero, who was a very nice person, was being chased by the Emperor's vicious soldiers. He happened to make it and save his life by crossing this river with his horse. One thing that stuck in my mind was the story did not say if the hero took his clothes off before he got in the water. Because the etiquette I was raised with was that you should take good care of anything you had so later you do not ask for more. I definitely believed that this nice hero of the story did not cross the river with his clothes on. So here was my first drawing. So I wanted to make sure that the teacher knows that I know that the hero undressed nicely on the bank and then he crossed the river. To make sure the teacher gets that I drew a pair of pants and a shirt plastered against the sky. Then it occurred to me that he would have to run nude on the other side when he finished swimming. So I solved this problem just by leaving this hero's head in the water scene and left the rest to the teacher to figure out what he did after he got to the other side. My friend Emel loved it. She giggled and knew the guy will look funny if he ever got out of the water. She asked me how is he going to go to his village without clothes? I told her that he has to go find a fig tree and go home like Adam did.

The last drawing in that class I made was a very sad one. This was the last story in our Alphabet Book. The story was about a mother bird that went to bring some food for its newly born very pretty babies. But this bad boy who had no good spirit shot the mother bird with his sling shot thinking that was cool and heroic. The story went on as the baby chicks began to cry "Mother! Mother, where are you?" But darkness set and the mother never came back and the baby birds could never leave the nest to go look for her since they had not yet been taught how to fly. That was the last of the stories before we left for summer break. Everybody was so sad. Emel almost cried and I tried to console her, and gave her a hug. When I looked up I saw the face of my tough teacher Madame Rabia with a look of a lost gaze, a portrait I will never forget, a sad and gentle face of humility and communion.

By my third year at school I was beginning to get mixed messages from the elders. The city -- as I mentioned -- was about sixty thousand in population and was totally contained within high walls built millenniums past as defense from migrant warrior tribesmen. The city had two gates. One was called the Mountain Gate and on the other side was the Gate of Mardin. The three thousand year old city with very rich historical resources: literally frozen in history. My father had bought the house of a Pasha "Ottoman District Ruler," after the collapse of the Empire in 1923. My mother, Mdm. Jozefine, with French upbringing liked to add a bit of modernity to the structure. Almost every day in the course of excavation the workers would find artifacts that were buried for centuries in the dirt. The law was that the municipal authorities had to be informed of any finding and since the police station did not have a phone I was the messenger in charge to run to the police station to inform them of any new discovery. The workers had to carefully pull out the object, an urn, a stone sculpture, a clay pot, or whatever, and wait for the police to pick it up. Because of these roles bestowed upon me I knew every corner of the city. I began to pick up languages and mannerisms. Even though I was constantly reminded of being a Christian which most locals referred to as the "Gavur" meaning, "INFIDEL" in Turkish; we had to be more conscious of our activities which I felt was under constant scrutiny. Thusly I learned to behave like a Muslim in the Muslim sector, a Jew in the Jewish sector, Armenian in the Armenian sector and an Arab or a Kurd when in their domain.

Only on Sundays, I could not be who and where I wanted to be. I had an important position and task. I was an alter boy. This position was very demanding but it had its rewards and incentives. Besides the assurance of having a place in heaven there was the "wine." The six alter boys who were there first, lined up on the right side of the alter. While the boys on the left were to handle the candles, the bell and the Holy Book, the ones on the right were in charge of the holy sacraments and wine which was to be fetched at the right time from the back of the alter. Well, the built-in privilege was to take care of the leftover wine after the ceremonies properly. Guess what? Since you could not put the leftover wine back in the vessel it came from, the boys took turns to properly evaluate the blood of Christ. I venture to say no one ever brought this sin to the attention of the priest during the regularly mandated confession. But we dispelled that by privately reciting three Ave Marias and three Pater Nostres.

But as they say, "you eventually pay." Since we had mustered the chutzpah to access the wine that was not meant for alter punks, I also often tasted the unbottled wine that was in huge ceramic containers in our cellar that my father was so proud of. One day I happened to be present and overheard that my father was pledging a monetary gift to the church. At a time when I thought it was proper, I told my dad not to give what he was pledging to the church council. I was surprised at his facial disapproval that is very familiar among the Mediterranean cultures to gesture communication mode highly popular especially in presence of outsiders. He took me to his chamber and asked me why I thought that he should not help the church. After forcing my hand I told him that I think the church does not need his money because they were richer than him. He asked me how I arrived to such a conclusion. He insisted so much that finally I had to tell him. "Dad," I said, "the priest's wine is much better than yours." He looked at me and said, "How do you know that?" I realized then and there that there is definitely God, that there was no escape, that it was time to pay.

To get a feeling that the elders felt that you can be given responsibilities which gave one a sense of power that you can deal with givens more readily and positively than those who were uncaring and irresponsible. We are the coconspirators in designating our own path of life and the major player of our destiny.

TALAS AMERICAN
SCHOOL FOR BOYS

One of the first American schools established overseas during the rule of the Ottoman Empire was TALAS, the beginning of my exposure to the American culture.

I will never forget my first encounter with a real American. All I knew and learned from exported cinema images in my elementary years was that America was a cowboy country. I really enjoyed the rough gunslingers of the West that were always on the move and the good guy always won. That unforgettable day our teacher walked in with a tall blond person. As usual to display respect we all stood up and waited for the teacher to order us to sit. She told us we have an American guest, whose name was Mr. Paul Nelson, who will ask some of us questions. I kept looking at him thinking he may be a homeless cowboy. If he is; he must need some help.

Well, after school I found out that he stayed as a guest at a family acquaintance with whose kid I regularly played. Since our parents taught us that we have to help those who may need help, I went to that house and knocked on the door. My friend's mother opened the door and asked me to come in. I asked her if Mr. Nelson was there and she pleasantly indicated that he was. She called on him and he came to see what it was all about. When he saw me he was very surprised and told the hostess that this was the boy he was telling them about. He was very pleased and asked me to come meet his wife. I was literally shocked. I did not think cowboys were married since they were poor. I said nothing but in my confused state of mind not knowing how I could possibly help this American with a wife, I told them that my parents would like to have them over for dinner on Sunday after Church. They were very pleased. My parents had no idea I had invited a poor cowboy and his wife to attend the monthly congregational dinner with the usual community elders.

After I left I went home and I do not recall exactly how I informed my mom that with my help they have invited an American to visit with them on Sunday after Church. To my surprise my mom thought that it was very nice of me to invite the Americans and indicated that my dad will appreciate my thoughtfulness.

Well, Mr. and Mrs. Nelson showed up and in the course of very engaging dialogues with my Dad, Mr. Nelson recommended that his son, me, who had highly impressed him in the course of his brief visit to my class and would get a very good education if he attended this very select Prep School hidden in the high peaks of Mount Erciyas in Central Turkey. These peaks, the adolescent boys soon determined resembled breasts.

My dad was surprised at the suggestion of his American guest. He was not very much interested because traditionally all who desired to acquire the real proper education was to pursue the French mode of academics. As I was listening it occurred to me that this American's recommendation was ideal for me. Since no one spoke English in the family I figured in a format like this I could totally avoid any daily review of my schoolwork. I would be free from all that tedious nonsense. I realized that all I had to do is convince the "Minister of the Interior," my Mom. She had the last word. The following day, I said my three Ave Marias and three Patre Nostres and approached her with every possible positive reason why at least one kid in the family could attend a different type of school. To my surprise, my prayers worked and after a few more convincing factors shared by other member of the family I was granted the conditional approval to attend this highly recognized prep school if my qualifications would fulfill the school's enrollment requirement and they will accept me.

I had no idea of where I was heading. I prayed to God the following Sunday that it be what I had envisioned. After going through the necessary procedures even I was surprised at the news that I was accepted.

All members of my extended family could not believe that I was going to be sent to a school far away from my hometown. It was not even a French School. My cousins were asking me a lot of questions about this faraway place. I had no idea. I only knew it was somewhere in the highest of Mount Erciyas near the center of Turkey. Anyway, the day for such a strange endeavor had arrived. All my family members showed up at the train station to bid my dad and myself good luck and best wishes. I felt like a hero going on a world expedition at age eleven. My dad, who had reserved a sleeping compartment on the Orient Express that ran from Syria to Constantinople, today's Istanbul, was escorting me. We were treated like royalty in the course of two days and two nights travel towards the city Turks called Kayseri. I had heard it was an ancient city where according to history the Roman emperor in the first century fearing the impact of a new cult called Cristianus that was disturbing the established order, of his empire arranged the deportation of the followers to the central planes of Anatolia. Thusly the geographic location was referred to as Cessarea, Ceaser's land. Centuries later the location came to be called Kayseri.

Two days later we arrived at the station. I was very excited but nervous. I did not know we had yet an hour ride to get to this mountain village. We had to wait awhile to find transportation that was willing to take us there. We finally found a cab and headed to the mysterious site. We arrived more than an hour later at the old campus that housed 187 select students from all around. I had mixed feelings. It really looked like the orphanage in my town. My father took me inside. We were directed to the administration office where we met Mr. Scott, the principal. After we had a brief protocol reception, my father thanked everyone and we walked out to the schoolyard. When we came out, the cab driver had unloaded my luggage and wanted to depart before it got dark. I hugged my dad and kissed him good-bye. And that was the beginning, at this "school of deportees," of my exposure to western cultural.

Here, miles away from home, I learned to earn my social security. This was truly an organic laboratory of self-identification. I was indeed blessed to be one of the boys in this form where we learned the meaning of interdependency and collaboration. This was not a social contract that we were born into as at home where everything was a given. Here we had to earn our personage. Due to such healthy social, academic and cultural interaction we learned what true bonding was. Now, at this last phase of our lives we all are a family at different addresses around the planet -- this ambassadors-at-large to share and contribute to the cultivation of humanity with all the resources we were blessed to have available to us.

Thus I got the chance to validate my grandfather's advice for those who were self-oriented, "Share what you have in the bag for you will take nothing with you when your time comes."

Ever since this wise dictum, I have gathered all information availed to me into a pot to make a healthy soup to be shared by all my acquaintances in a timely fashion.

IN VITIUM DUCIT
CULPAE FUGA

Horatius

Displeasures Of End-Oriented Cultures: Warrior Gengis Khan And The Village Marksman

In fear of misconduct we exercise guilt.
We partake in crime in fear of misconduct.

Maazeretleri kiymeti yoktur, kiymetler neticelerdedir

A Turkish Proverb

Excuses carry no value; values lie in the ends.

In the course of my higher academic endeavors at Tarsus American College in Tarsus, Turkey, the hometown of St. Paul, I had an interesting awakening.

One day, I was sitting in a classroom taking an analytic geometry exam in middle school, during the times when some of us had access to slide rules instead of calculators. As I tried to scale my slide rule to solve one of the problems, I heard my teacher, Mr. Hans Meyer, step down from the lecture podium and come over to me and asked me what I was doing. I told him I was trying to solve the problem. He looked at me and said, "I am not interested in the answer, I am very much interested in how you arrive at it."

Nowadays more and more cultures value the ends rather then the means. The reason one studies history is to learn not repeat the bad experiences of the past. However in the course of time man has greatly suffered due to unnecessary inner fear of social acceptability. Due to this fear man has put most of his energy into mastering a deceptive exposure.

I remember as a kid reading a story about the ancient Turkish warrior Cengiz Han known as Genghis Khan by contemporary western cultures. The fable was that he was the best archer in the known lands. One could draw a circle and from any distance he would hit the bull's eye. But one day as he was riding with his men through a forest, he saw trees with an arrow perfectly in the middle of a red circle. He asked his man to find out who this person was and bring him to His Majesty immediately. The horsemen charged into the nearest village and asked about the identity and the whereabouts of this person who has such talent to match their master. Why, he is the eight-year-old Orhan. They located the boy and took him to the Master Warrior. Cengiz Han asked him if he was the one who had all these arrows in the bull's eyes. The boy answered, "Yes, there is nothing to it. Anyone can if they follow my way." The Master Worrier said, "Show me." The boy got an arrow and set it in the bow without any hesitation just shot at the tree. Then he walked to it and took out a piece of dry red clay from his pocket and drew a circle around the arrow he had just shot. Cengiz Han in shock looked and could not believe that this little boy had achieved the same goal with absolutely no effort.

Today I see many people who have mastered drawing the circle after the shot who pretend that they have gone through a lot to reach that goal which seems so unreachable by average standards.

How sad that those who continuously complain about their lives which lack substance do not realize that they are the perpetrators of the false images they have released to those they want to connect with. They do not realize that any connection they have achieved through a false presentation no matter how convincing will eventually come to haunt them.

This leads to the element most destructive to human creativity: **fear.**

UDUM ET MOLLE LUTUM EST, NUNC PROPERANDUS, ET ACRI FINGEDUS SINE FINE ROTA

Persius

The clay damp and soft; we have to hurry
The ever rotating wheel should give it its form.

All man's fear could vastly be diminished and understood, eliminated, if they learned to respond to givens in a timely fashion. Clay could be better molded when fresh. Early cultures paid attention and learned a lot by observing the ordinary behavior of nature. Greeks have a saying; "A tree can bend when it is young and fresh." Ironically, as the Greeks and Turks have experienced centuries of social conflict, the Turks have a similar saying, "A tree that resists bending to the will of the wind is destined to break." So what is the correlation? What did Persius hint by his observation?

There is a right time for every human engagement. It is easier to teach a child a new idea than an older person. Therefore it is easier to cultivate a young mind than an older one. Resistance comes when the perceiver of an idea has missed the opportunity to process the information necessary to comprehend what is served. When this happens, the saying above activates its meaning. When one has not learned to respond to the harsh wind, one fails to bend to its direction and thus suffers a break. This explanation sounds harsh. But, here is the reality. Only a prepared and educated mind can direct the destructive energy of the wind to its advantage; that is, to deal with harsh opposition because it knows it is temporary and the educated mind – like the branch will eventually be restored to its normal position again. Chinese self-defense discipline is basically a result of this natural principle. The well-trained bullfighter is hailed only when he elegantly deflects the destructive power of the bull upon itself and defeats it.

FALSE PRESENCE
A SOCIETY OF TAKERS
THEN MAKERS

Reaping The Fields Sowed By Others

"Inasmuch as most things are produced by labor, it follows that all such things ought to belong to those whose labor has produced them. But it has happened in all ages of the world that some have labored, and others without labor, have enjoyed a larger proportion of the fruits. This is wrong and should not continue. To secure to each laborer the whole product of his labor as nearly as possible is a worthy object of any good government."

> Abraham Lincoln (From first annual message to Congress, December 3, 1861.)

Somehow, due to ignorance, history keeps repeating itself. As the French saying goes, "Plus les change, plus de la mem chose." The more change the more things stay the same. The Roman senators - I heard from my history teacher in middle school - were getting luxurious compensation but they never went to the senate to deal with problems of the people. They were in the market wheeling and dealing in every corrupt exchange from stolen goods to buying and selling slaves and blending with the rest in the market with their white outfits. We heard that the reason Caesar was killed by a group of senators, including Brutus, was that he had issued an ordinance that all senators had to wear purple on their togas. This would identify them to the centurions who would bring them to the senate floor where they were paid to be and to serve the people they pretended to represent.

We see the same reflection of disgust by Sir Thomas Moore, in Utopia (1516), "There is a great number of noblemen among you that are themselves as idle as drones that subsist on other men's labor, on the labor of their tenants, who raise their own resources they pare to the quick. Besides this, they carry about with them a great number of idle fellows, who never learned any trade by which they may gain a living, and these, as soon as their lord dies, are turned out of doors. Those turned out of doors grow keen and they rob no less keenly, for what else can they do?"

A while back as I was attending a political fundraising for a senator at a posh golf outing in suburban Chicago, I could not believe what I experienced as I was walking through the main meeting room of this club. The senator who was enjoying his champagne before the outing was introduced as "live" on one of the major networks delivering a highly vested image of concern of the issue on the floor as if he was really there. All were enjoying their cocktail with him laughing and commending him for his production of a false presence. I turned to him and said, "Sir, if what I am seeing on the screen is live we must be enjoying this moment with a dead senator." Even he found it highly humorous by responding, "Hey that is what makes a good politician. To have the power to be wherever you think you should be."

I hear many so-called social leaders on talk shows advocate artificial presence. Because of such artificial advocacies many have mastered how to share the benefits of others deserving benefits of their lifetime dedications. They are encouraged to be successful at any cost. False pretense of input by many is nowadays considered smart and productive. When I hear of the promotions of some to posts that they admit they acquired because they knew how to take advantage of somebody else's hard work, I think that I was blessed that I got my life ethics through exposure to a culture equipped to feed complex social ideals through simple humor which for a child was much easier to swallow and digest. Related to the ethics of compensation for false presence and demand of compensation for superficial input that you hear everyday from the leaders reminds me of the story of the village woodcutter.

There was an old woodcutter. For many years this very hardworking man left the village every day to go chop wood in a nearby forest and bring it to the bazaar to sell. One day as he was walking to the woods, he saw a man who was known as the town wheeler-dealer follow him. He did not say anything. He arrived at the forest, took out the ax that he had sharpened the night before and realized that the man was sitting in a nice shady spot. The woodcutter began to chop at the tree, but every time he flung a blow with his ax, he heard the man utter a loud, sound "Ughf!!!" He did not know what the man was doing but he continued to cut enough to take to the market. All the while the man kept up the huffing sound until the woodcutter finished cutting what he can carry on his donkey.

The woodcutter headed for the bazaar, unloaded his load and began to sell the bundles when he realized that the man that had followed him had come and crouched by him. He tried to ignore the man. Well before the day was over, he sold all he had cut. As he was about to get on his donkey and leave the market, the strange fellow approached him and told the woodcutter that half of the money he had made selling the wood was his. The woodcutter looked at him totally confused and asked him how he came up with such a ridiculous idea. The man said to him, yes you cut the wood; but I helped you by making all the huffing sound you needed for proper cutting. The woodcutter was outraged at such a stand. The man threatened the woodcutter and told him that if he did not give him half of what he got for the wood, he would sue him. The woodcutter could not believe that this man had the audacity to ask for half of what he worked for. So he refused to give him anything and walked away.

A few days later a court's messenger came and told the woodcutter he had to appear in the presence of local Hoca, a religious arbitrator. He could not eat and sleep, and the following morning he went to the Hoca's court. The man presented his case. He said, "Your highness, I went with this man all the way to the woods where he does his cutting. I was with him all the while he cut the wood." The Hoca asked him, "What did you do to think that you deserve half of the benefits of this hard work?" "Your honor I released the best "huff." at every swing of his axe. I did not miss one." The Hoca turned to the woodcutter and asked if what this man said was true. The woodcutter respectfully agreed. The Hoca looked at the astonished woodcutter and said, "Well, the man has a point. He must get his deserved share." The woodcutter could not believe what he was hearing from this supposedly spiritual judge. The Hoca reached for a metal tray, walked to the woodcutter and told him to empty the bag of coins into the metal tray. The woodcutter obliged. The falling coins from the bag made a pinging sound as they poured. The Hoca turned to the man and asked him, "Did you hear that fantastic sound of the shekels?" The man said, "Yes your honor." "Well! We are getting somewhere. Sir," said the Hoca, "the sound you heard is yours. The rest goes to the woodcutter."

CONTENT AND CONTAINER

The Road To Self-Acceptance

"In me omnis speat est mihi"

Terentius

"All what I wish is in me."

We were taught very early that one should never condition one's happiness or the truth that one holds dear by the opinions of others. Thus one can learn a lot from rules and values held by past cultures. Their successes and failures are maps for future routes to be taken.

"Who deserves the honor?"

Sufi Nasraddin

The entry into any social format has been not the acquisition of proper social input but the artificial presence of the facade.

I will never forget the story I was told about a village philosopher. This old man who had spent most of his life helping those in need of sound advice for the betterment of their lives. In the course of his social dedication he had helped a man to get out of financial trouble and to succeed. One day the man he had helped to overcome his miserable past with his recently acquired wealth decided to celebrate his success by inviting all the village leaders to a very festive evening.

The philosopher arrived wearing his every-day clothes to this important dinner. The butler at the door did not recognize him. So they gave him a seat near the door quite far from the host. At one point he thought that he would go and congratulate the host on his success. He was very disappointed when he realized the man he had helped to become who he was did not recognize him. He then walked back towards his seating place and avoiding any notice gracefully exited. He went home and put on an elegant outfit that he had not worn for years and came back to the dinner hall. The host saw this most elegantly dressed man enter, but he still did not recognize who he was. Impressed by the grand outfit the host got up and extended an impressive welcome and requested the guest to join him at his table.

As the host tried to initiate a conversation with his new guest, the host to his amazement realized the guest was stuffing the food from the table into his pockets. The host could not believe his eyes. After resisting any form of shame and humiliation, he asked, "Sir, who are you and why are you stuffing all that food into the pockets of such elegant clothes?" The guest turned to the host and said, "You do not recognize me, do you? I am Sufi Nasraddin. I came here for the sole purpose to celebrate your success because you had once told me that your success was due to the education and wisdom you got from me. Do you recall promising that you will always remember to honor and respect those with inner rather than outer reflections? Without these clothes you did not recognize me. Now tell me, with all of your wealth and wisdom. Who really deserves all this festive food? Me or the impressive outfit that enabled me to gain a high seat next to you?"

POWER & HUMANITY

Humanity vs. Physicality

"And the rest rose to their feet, the sceptered kings,
obeying the shepherd of the people, and the army thronged
behind them"

Homer, The Iliad

In the middle ages, the Stoics believed that to make the best of one's life it was imperative to exercise moral conduct. When one exercises moral conduct one opens the door to the essentials of self-composure.

The works of hardly remembered seventeenth-century philosopher, thinker and educator, John Amos Comenius of Moravia, were translated into dozens of languages, including Turkish, Arabic, Persian, Mongolian and many others. His most impressive work, "Orbis Sensualium Pictus," "The World Portrayed to the Senses," impressed many intellectuals including the likes of Locke and Milton. Many of our present and future developing minds could greatly benefit from the following commentary.

"I began to concentrate my designs upon an endeavor to reconcile the whole human race. If men were shown what

their complete and real good is, they will be drawn to it. Where they, moreover, shown the right means for its achievement, an all-inclusive and all -satisfying philosophy, religion and statecraft would be finally attained."

J.A. Comenius (c. 1600).

Today, a big portion of educational resources is diverted towards façade-oriented engagements, the so-called "physical education" and comparatively little for the arts and humanities. An individual is nothing but a total byproduct of the community he was brought into. It does not take, as the saying goes, a rocket scientist, to recognize a culture that fails to develop the mind and the spirit for proper social engagement instead of turning them into organic offensive weapons that are destined for ruin.

Ironically, too often in the socio pomoable that offensive, mindless, toughness is called "cool." How would a developing mind translate the values of our leaders in their resource allocation in education, when they see that they invest huge amounts into sports and next to nothing in the most essential ingredients for intellectual, cultural and spiritual development. Visual, literary and performing arts in the West get the least amount of attention. A football coach at a leading university in the Midwest I have heard that is being paid over a million dollars a year plus other bonuses surpassing the total compensation of seven academicians in the humanities department.

THE SHARPER THE SWORD
THE TOUGHER THE
INTELLECTUAL SHIELD

In 1901, at the Minnesota State fair, then Vice President Theodore Roosevelt uttered his famous foreign policy advice, "Speak softly and carry a big stick," it resonated positively with those who understood the true inference of it.

The root of that statement originated from the old Greek philosopher Aristophanes. Often - even in ancient Mesopotamian cultures - it was preached that only an educated and cultured mind is capable of developing a soft tongue to avoid the big stick. In the course of human history, societies that vested in intellectual and spiritual resources tended to have more social acceptability by their neighbors in the socio-political arena. In almost all political conflict the society that had the most awareness of not only their cultural history but also the cultural weaknesses and strengths of other cultures had a better chance to prevail.

The Huns, the ferocious warriors of Turkish origin led by Attila, who had the power to conquer any land they marched into, including Rome in 395 AD, had no clue of the importance of the cultural resources that they could have benefited from. Attila was very easily manipulated by the soft tongue of the Pope who had a better understanding of dealing with a brain that believed in the power of the big stick. Whereas another warrior tribe from the same roots led by Osman and his descendents - one of whom happened to be Suleyman - inherited the title the "Magnificent" for initiating laws that unified the multiple cultures within the domain of the longest surviving empire (1150 to 1919), the "Ottoman."

The word "Ottoman" in the West, known only as nothing but a piece of furniture, actually was derived from the same culture. In the Turkish language the "divan" was a chamber established for the sole purpose of socio-cultural exchange through literature and letters.

The leaders of this Turkish culture benefited extensively by the creation of an intercultural chamber where members of the nations that they ruled met regularly to discuss and share their tribal values through poetry and prose. This format created one of the richest literary heritages known by many as "Divan Edebiyati," laid the foundation for the rich cultural forum as "Ottoman Literature."

Better as Greco-Roman then just as Roman

I recall that when my brother was attending primary school his report card indicated that he was not doing well. When my mom questioned the reasoning, he insisted that he did not understand what all the fuss was about. He told her he was the best soccer player of his class. I was just at an age to attend the same school. Mom looked at both of us and said, "Now both of you sit and listen to me very carefully. I am going to share with you a historical secret. You both have heard about the famous Romans and their gladiators. They put all their attention in building their bodies, but forgot to educate their mind. Where are they now? They are gone. They do not exist anymore. The Greeks on the other hand emphasized the mind, but forgot the body. So they suffered by those with brainless bodies. So both of you have to see that you grow up as Greco-Roman. Because a brainless body tends to exercise offense and physically weak brain always seeks defense. When you grow up you will find out that with an educated mind and well-maintained body you will have more of a chance to live a happy and productive life. So if you want to live a socially-acceptable life and receive the admiration of your peers and elders you have to see that you grow up to be mentally equipped and physically fit citizens." Years later while in high school, I remember thinking my awareness of the law of gravity must have helped me win first place in pole vaulting and get elected Chairman of the Student Court. Then I realized that my mother's observation and teachings laid the groundwork for my future as an advocator of proper use of human resources through the arts.

ARTS: ETHICS FREE ZONE

Marketing Offense As Defense Of Humanity

The arts in the history of man have been channeled in many forms and dimensions. But the inherent values have always been for the betterment of mankind. Due to the many restrictive factors initiated by the insecure power holders, the complex statements were released through very carefully composed fine and entertaining modes of covert delivery. Thus when the arts are presented with the intent of sharing essential life values through enjoyable social aesthetics, they have always been referred to as "fine arts."

When the arts are intentionally misused for the sole purpose of marketing trash camouflaged as entertainment and engage in social manipulation and cultural degradation should they be referred to as "rough arts?"

Fine arts in the course of time have been used as aesthetically packaged statements that contain universal messages and commentaries for the sole purpose of creating awareness of the bad and the good that may not be pleasantly received by the holders of the sword if delivered openly. The arts often have been venues in availing the wisdom of survivorship through wise modes and rules for timely bending into direction of the wind to maintain one's roots

THE OAK VS. THE REED

Aesop

One day in my elementary school courtyard this tough looking boy was bragging to a little boy sitting next to him that his Asian ancestors were the toughest warriors that beat every tribe they ran into. This verbal intimidation went on and on 'til the bell rang and the little boy and all who were listening were relieved to get up and run to attend class. Ironically that same day the teacher happened to introduces us to Aesop's wisdom by reading us a story. She began to read.

"One day an oak tree called on a tall gentle reed that stood across the creek and tried to engage into an intimidating argument of who was the strongest among all living plants. The reed tried to ignore the oak and tried to enjoy watching the beautiful and colorful flow of the river and the creatures swimming in it. The oak tree went on and on bragging about its gigantic size and the power of its clenching roots. As the lecture of the oak got harsher a very strong wind came up blowing in their direction. The reed having put more attention to educating itself about the nature that surrounded it, bent with the flow avoiding being uprooted, where the oak stood firm contesting the power of the wind. When the chaos was over the reed lifted its head and saw that the tough oak had been uprooted and totally destroyed."

When the teacher finished, the little boy sitting next to me bent over and signaled at the big tough boy and gave him a big smile and a funny "winners" look. Later on in the courtyard the boy came to a group of us sitting together and said, "We've got to read more of this Aesop fellow. He is really smart."

THE UNIVERSAL NEED TO COMMUNE BASIS OF THE TEN COMMANDMENTS

Six days shalt thou labour and do all thy work:

But the seventh day is the Sabbath of the Lord and thy God: in it thou shalt not do any work, thou nor thy son, nor thy daughter, thy manservant nor thy maidservant, nor thy cattle, nor thy stranger that is within thy gates:

"There is no hope of joy except in human relations"

Antoine de Saint Expure

Origins of Sharing of Bread and Water.

In the history of mankind one of the most essential elements that has contributed to human conflict has been the lack of open and healthy social interaction. One can easily review the observations and advocacy of this basic need by all philosophers, thinkers, and prophets of the past. Even long before the Abrahamic era, due to limited economic and life-sustaining resources, people had to be continuously on the move. Due to this of nomadic desert life, the only source of cultural interaction were brief communal gatherings. For that reason alone they came to the realization that it was imperative to learn about the lives and needs of other tribes that they encountered in the course of their mobility. If one takes a brief review, the prerequisites of all major theological teachings, one would observe the necessity for a special time designated for social communion. Why was this so necessary?

Cultures of the past did not have access to the vast economic resources that we have been availed to today. Is this vast accessibility really a blessing or a curse? I, as a student of humanities, tend to hold my reservations. When one reviews even the monotheistic cultures, social conflicts began to present themselves when people failed to observe the Sabbath, the seventh day of the week for the sole purpose of getting to commune by sharing their limited bread and water. In the beginning there was no such place called a "Temple." Then this basic need to commune for the sole purpose of social adjustment and inter-tribal forum eventually developed into a spiritual arena, which today is recognized as a temple, church or mosque.

Later we learn that a certain member of the temple who really believed in the essence of this practice got to be excommunicated for simply admonishing those who had turned the Center of communal and spiritual therapy into a marketing arena of goods and services. Those who followed the honest and true importance of the weekly social interaction were called by the temple leaders as "Cristianus" in Greek "the tainted ones." Thusly the true believers of this social need dedicated themselves to meet and interact on the first day of the week, Sunday.

A few centuries later they again began to neglect this necessary social practice. Realizing the importance of such a format for social connectivity and the avoidance of cultural conflict an Arabian culture began to congregate on Friday. In Arabic it is called the "Cum'a", the Communal Day. Originally those congregation sites were just locations easy to get to by any member of the tribe. It could have been a cave, a tent or any shaded enclave definitely better if close to a water source. This gave the participants an awareness of the need to share the life essentials that came to be the foundation of all future religions. Unfortunately the universal symbols of bread and water have been taken out of context by cultures that mastered the ways and means of wealth and the power of acquisition without the original basis for appreciation.

I find it highly ironic that even with such limited resources those cultures before the Greeks and Romans realized the importance of sharing anything that they were accessed to. All the cultural rules and social regulations that contemporary cultures wish to exercise were inherited through the teachings derived from the meaningful sayings, poems, stories and proverbs of nomadic tribes with limited economic resources.

Arts: The basis for advocacy of leisure.

As cultures became economically self-sufficient they began to be less mobile and more resolute in creating a domain that gave them the opportunity to be the host to many mobile cultures just as they used to be. Having the knowledge of the importance of basic economic needs they began to channel their excessive resources to express their social values through carefully and aesthetically enjoyable visual images. Sometimes they carved some sayings that contained the symbols not only of their social ethics but universally appreciated values.

This manner of delivery of the arts was not to just enhance the grandeur of their estates, but it was a way of sharing with their visitors their past so they could better appreciate their present and assure the healthy and productive lives of their future generations.

A CULTURE FAILING TO DISTINGUISHING COMEDY FROM TRAGEDY --STUDY BEFORE YOU SAY--

"Art is a window to eternity."

Due to the reality of limited resources the artist of the past had to make sure that when he hit the chisel it was to help carve the image to make the statement he had studied and thus believed in its communal impact.

I sometimes wonder if we could invite the cultural contributors of the past such as Dante, Boccaccio, Ariosto, Ruben, Mevlana, Luther, Mozart, Dostoyevski, and Mark Twain to see what they think of our arts. I believe they would all agree that we have created a generation that is totally disconnected from the realities of true and healthy living.

It is very unfortunate that with all our economic advantages, we sadly have generated a lifestyle that has blinded many in defining the real purpose of their presence on this human canvas. Due to the fast forward lifestyle the contemporary forums of connectivity have been reduced to empty, destructive and artificial images poured into the young developing minds as socially acceptable.

The universal forms to channeling the humanistic values literary, performing, and visual arts have totally been neglected. We have become a most published and unfortunately the least read society marketing itself as leading universalists.

One wonders about what branch of the arts no other then fast revenue-generating venue that requires no basic social knowledge of any kind for mass attendance do mind benders and cultural social parasites of our generation invest into? The answer is cinema and televised visual crafts.

Why cinema? Because in the contemporary social environment it requires no preconditions to partake. Instead of developing the required basics for cohesive life for the so called creative mind to be able to express a universal sophisticated theme within one frame as by such Renaissance artists, such as Duerer, Giovanni Bellini, Leonardo da Vinci, Vittore Carpacio, Hieronymus Bosch, this contemporary form of visual arts with such possibilities, which originally was used to make very engaging and sophisticated statements, has entered into an era of failure. The technological accessibilities of our times has failed to even make a simple and culturally productive statement by choosing to glue billions of frames together for fast, empty and corrosive entertainment.

So how have the so-called "producers" turned the basic foundation of visual and performing arts from statement-making to fast mass-marketing? Simple, no sophisticated theme is necessary. Since there is no story the most destructive and offensive role goes to the lead as hero who carries the biggest stick and roughest tongue. The story is simply a senseless, rough interaction among those with the toughest bodies with empty craniums. The hero is he who is most capable of abusing the space of other contesting abusers.

Would not a young mind deduce that a highly powerful body with offensive and invasive behavior is socially acceptable? Should a culture availed with all resources not make use of such an impressive art form to differentiate offense from defense?

Ironically we never learn from simple ancient stories. As children we learned that it was not David who entered into an un-welcomed space of others but it was the giant brutal Goliath. Who won the battle? The little boy who used his brain won the battle; not the monster Goliath with his offensive and invasive presence.

How could a child continuously exposed to images blended with senseless sound bites of toughness and universally unacceptable offensive physical behavior assimilate proper human conduct? As an international artist, I wonder about how all these register with even mildly educated minds around the globe view our society with all the God-given wealth markets such offensive images as socially approved values through its arts?

When the body with underdeveloped mind has to be quite insecure since it has difficulty comprehending what is going on around it. Could this possibly lead to communal suspension, which may possibly lead to unnecessary offensive and invasive behavior?

Not only does contemporary western society advocate senseless physicality but also it openly misuses available art forms and feeds it to the developing minds as acceptable behavior. Then the same leaders who financially benefit from misusing such human resources approach the public surprised and disgusted in the news of increasing violence exercised upon the society by idle minds whose values are derived through the media arts they consciously market?

BIRI YER BIRI BAKAR, KIYAMET BUNDAN DOGAR

"One eats and one looks, thusly havoc cooks."

Ancient Turkish proverb

The man who lead the salvaging of the remnants of the most powerful empire that iron-handedly ruled cultures on three continents for centuries, Mustafa Kemal Ataturk spoke to his followers in 1923: "My friends, those who conquer by sword are doomed to be overcome by those who conquer with the plough, and finally give a place to them. That is what happened to the Ottoman Empire. The arm that wields the sword grows weary and in the end puts it back in the scabbard, where perhaps it is doomed to corrode and molder, but the arm that holds the plough grows daily stronger and in growing stronger becomes yet more the master and the owner of the land."

Learning to be cultivators in any field has been the main aim of all cultures that have experienced social crisis. Social, economic and cultural cultivation opens the gates for collective access to the socio economic resources. When there is only one loaf of bread to be shared by a family of twenty, what conscious heart would justify giving half of the loaf to one member and the other half to be shared by the rest? This is a question that is being asked around the globe. Whose God could come with a convincing ethos to praise this one overweight member of the family that claims to be the advocate of human rights, yet consumes almost everything that is on the table. Why is it that all throughout history cultures who have grown rich and powerful somehow fail to look back and see how they felt when they were the servants of those they conquered. How they felt when their overweight self-declared master ate most of the butter they brought to the table by simply holding the big gun. It is time to wake up and put the remote control aside and listen to those who are the real witnesses of the real truth and universally recognized reality.

THE GUN VERSES THE PEN

Moral courage versus mortal conquest

In my recollection of my studies of any conflict in world history, nowhere do I recall that the last weapon used in any conflict was the gun. Even though I hear a lot of threat and tough talk. One has to admit that every worldly conflict ends with the triumph of the pen. You have heard that one can win the battle but loose the war. If that is possible than it is conceivable that one can loose the battle and win the war. In either case the victim is the obeying soldier who never gets to benefit from either outcome. Then who is the beneficiary? Could it be the leader protected in a fortified undiscoverable location falsely marketed as an honorable hero, benefits from the sustained human tragedy?

I venture to say people of this planet need to learn early in life to recognize their voids and share with others the excesses that may be sitting idle to be part of the social composition. In history the gun has always made its presence when one offends the space and values of others. So if that holds any truth it is essential that everybody learn to show some respect to those who have made the effort to learn how to live on this planet by harvesting only what they have planted.

The winning of the gun is highly ephemeral. If philosophers and social thinkers make use of chapter one of Economics 101 they could make use of the symbolism of basic economics, gun verses butter. Would it not be unwise to eliminate the limited life resources just to promote and portray their weak ego? Russians have a saying that every child in third world countries recite. It goes, "A hungry bear will never dance." Which means that even animals like to be fed before they can have fun. But what have they done since 1917? The resources that were supposed to go towards the sickle, a symbol that stood for farming cultivation were pounded to pulp by the hammer. Thus to avoid social chaos, the pen was put under house arrest. Many social advocators of human rights, free self-expression, believed that Leo Tolstoy cried from his grave till the pen came out as the winner.

BETTER ALONE THAN POORLY ACCOMMODATED

Polonius' Advice To His Son

These few percepts in thy memory
See thou character. Give thy thoughts no tongue,
Nor any unproportioned thought his act.
Be thou familiar, but by no means vulgar:
The friends thou hast, and their adoption tried,
Grapple them to, thy soul with hoops of steel;
But do not dull thy palm with entertainment.
Of each new hatch'd unfledg'd comrade. Beware
Of entrance to the quarrel: but being in,
Bear't that th' opposed may beware of thee.
Give every man thine ear, but few thy voice:
Take each man' censure, but reserve thy judgment.
Costly thy habit as thy purse can buy,
But not express'd in fancy: rich, gaudy;
For the apparel oft proclaim the man.
Neither a borrower nor a lender be;
For loan oft loses both itself and friend,
And borrowing dulls the edge of husbandry.
This above all: to thine own self be true:
And it must follow, as the night the day,
Thou canst not then be false to any man.

Hamlet

HOME FOR SALE?

"I learned at last, what Home could be
How ignorant I had been
Of pretty ways of Covenant
How awkward the Hymn

Round our new Fireside, but for this-
This pattern; of the Way-
Whose memory drowns me,
Like the Dip of the Celestial Sea

What morning in our garden; guessed
What bees for us to hum
With only birds to interrupt
The ripple of our Theme

And ask for both the problem of the brain
And mine some foolisher effect
A Ruffle or a Tune

The afternoons together spent
And Twilight, in the Lanes
Some ministry to poorer lives
Seen poorest thro' our Gains

An then return a night and Home
An then ways to you to pass
A new diviner care
Till sunrise takes us back to the Scene
Transmuted Vivider

This seems a Home
And home is not
But what the place could be
Afflicts me as a Setting Sun
Where Dawn knows how to be."

Emily Dickenson

In the course of my early exposure to the North American culture a moment that got imbedded in my memory was a sign I read as I was driving through the streets of an upstate New York town. The sign was in front of a relatively huge house and read "HOME FOR SALE." I stopped and looked at it and read it carefully again. It did not make any sense. I did not get it. I asked myself, "Who in his right mind would and could sell his home?" To me from where I had come from a home was not the architectural structure but the collective social atmosphere that took years to form itself where one can feel a contributive and essential part. Those elements were not only the family members but the social, spiritual and cultural elements that created a bonding with a social track record. People in history moved only due to war or famine. Even then when people moved they may have left their house but they carry their home with them. But for some unexplainable reason today people move around not because of economic need but no other then image and acquisition of social status. One may buy the most grandiose house but one can never buy a home.

It is so unfortunate that our culture's propagation of economic wealth over communal engagements has rendered many physically accessed but spiritually homeless.

We're Deeply Alienated From Those Who Are Most Dear To Us

One day I heard my philosophy teacher saying that the culture he comes from believes that it is better to be alone then poorly accommodated. I always thought about that. Somehow I did not quite relate to that manner of belief. In my life experience I have come to realize that he who knows how to accommodate others is never alone. One can only sense his worth through his contributions not through his acquisitions.

Ironically it is the belief I have withdrawn from ancient thinkers that being overly accommodated lessens the creative process and human connectivity. It may be by many western minds considered as a form of prestige of accessibility to many houses but the real estate is nowhere else but one's home. The word "Real Estate" originally came from the old Aramaic word (gayre menkul) which roughly interpreted means (the unmovable). It was believed that one couldn't just carry and move their real-life home that took generations to nurture, to a new land and artificially-acquired estate. That is why in the past it was referred as "home."

My dear friends, home is where we can properly and fully appreciate all the spiritual, social and cultural wealth granted to us by our ancestors and a space within which we can feel and be a contributive part.

The time is now to learn how to enjoy all life's spices with gentle human elegance and not be a jackass and kick the gifts served to us on a plate. You know you are home when the vinegar in that old cup tastes better than any wine in a golden chalice you shared with those conquering warriors. We can better enjoy all that we receive if we have learned to give.

BEFORE BIDDING THE FINAL GOOD-BYE

Please come in
And be not shy
Join us all
As passers by

With gentle care
With all do share
A cup of water
And a piece of rye

In searching soul
The warm air
Mused in Joyous
Human flair

We thank those all
Who before us
Paced of drifting
Planted the seeds and
Did all the lifting
For us to enjoy
All God's gifting

Find a place
Which may comfort thee
And most befits
Your own pace
With no preclusion
Any color, form or race.

With love to all

Ano